U.S. Tort Liability for Large-Scale Artificial Intelligence Damages

A Primer for Developers and Policymakers

KETAN RAMAKRISHNAN, GREGORY SMITH, CONOR DOWNEY

For more information on this publication, visit **www.rand.org/t/RRA3084-1**.

About RAND

RAND is a research organization that develops solutions to public policy challenges to help make communities throughout the world safer and more secure, healthier and more prosperous. RAND is nonprofit, nonpartisan, and committed to the public interest. To learn more about RAND, visit www.rand.org.

Research Integrity

Our mission to help improve policy and decisionmaking through research and analysis is enabled through our core values of quality and objectivity and our unwavering commitment to the highest level of integrity and ethical behavior. To help ensure our research and analysis are rigorous, objective, and nonpartisan, we subject our research publications to a robust and exacting quality-assurance process; avoid both the appearance and reality of financial and other conflicts of interest through staff training, project screening, and a policy of mandatory disclosure; and pursue transparency in our research engagements through our commitment to the open publication of our research findings and recommendations, disclosure of the source of funding of published research, and policies to ensure intellectual independence. For more information, visit www.rand.org/about/research-integrity.

RAND's publications do not necessarily reflect the opinions of its research clients and sponsors.

Published by the RAND Corporation, Santa Monica, Calif.
© 2024 RAND Corporation
RAND® is a registered trademark.

Library of Congress Cataloging-in-Publication Data is available for this publication.
ISBN: 978-1-9774-1339-0

About This Report

This report describes the basic features of U.S. tort law and analyzes their significance for the liability of artificial intelligence (AI) developers whose models inflict, or are used to inflict, large-scale harm. The report is intended to be useful to AI developers, policymakers, and other nonlegal audiences (as well as lawyers) who wish to understand the liability exposure that AI development may entail, how this exposure might be mitigated, and how the existing liability regime might be improved by legislation in order to enhance its ability to properly incentivize responsible innovation.

Technology and Security Policy Center

RAND Global and Emerging Risks is a division of RAND that delivers rigorous and objective public policy research on the most consequential challenges to civilization and global security. This work was undertaken by the division's Technology and Security Policy Center, which explores how high-consequence, dual-use technologies change the global competition and threat environment, then develops policy and technology options to advance the security of the United States, its allies and partners, and the world. For more information, contact tasp@rand.org.

Funding

Funding for this work was provided by gifts from RAND supporters.

Author Affiliations

Ketan Ramakrishnan, an author of this report, is an associate professor of law at Yale Law School. Gregory Smith is a policy analyst at RAND. Conor Downey is a Ph.D. student at the Massachusetts Institute of Technology and a Technology and Security Policy fellow at RAND; for more information on the fellowship program, visit www.rand.org/tasp-fellows.

Members of the research team have family members who are executives at a major technology company. Neither these relations nor the company they work for had any input toward or influence on this report.

Acknowledgments

We would like to thank the leadership of the RAND Technology and Security Policy Center, Jeff Alstott and Emma Westerman, for their guidance on this publication; our senior adviser, James Anderson; and our reviewers, Karlyn Stanley of RAND and Mark Geistfeld, the Sheila Lubetsky

Birnbaum Professor of Civil Litigation at New York University School of Law, for their thoughtful reviews and helpful suggestions.

Summary

Leading artificial intelligence (AI) developers and researchers, as well as government officials and policymakers, are actively investigating and debating the harms that advanced AI systems might cause, including harms on a large scale.[1] In the future, many developers and researchers believe, advanced AI might be capable of creating (or facilitating the creation of) novel biological and chemical weapons;[2] empowering malicious actors or geopolitical adversaries of the United States to conduct powerful cyberattacks that destabilize critical economic, political, and military infrastructure;[3] and enabling wide-ranging and highly efficient phishing operations or other forms of theft and fraud.[4] In addition to being misused in these or other ways, advanced AI might *malfunction*, by behaving in an undesirable, unexpected, and harmful manner. So, for example, an advanced AI system might attempt to deceive humans online, without being prompted to do so by its user (or any other party).[5] Certain advanced AI systems might also cause havoc by propagating uncontrollably online, infecting computers and

---

[1] The governments of the United States, the United Kingdom, Australia, Canada, Chile, France, Germany, India, Indonesia, Israel, Italy, Japan, Kenya, Mexico, Netherlands, Nigeria, New Zealand, the Philippines, Republic of Korea, Rwanda, Kingdom of Saudi Arabia, Singapore, Spain, Switzerland, Türkiye, Ukraine, and the European Union have recently expressed concern about—and taken action to address—chemical, biological, radiological, nuclear, cybersecurity-related, and other risks posed by advanced AI systems. *See, e.g.*, Press Release, The White House, President Biden Issues Executive Order on Safe, Secure, and Trustworthy Artificial Intelligence (Oct. 30, 2023); U.K. Dept. of Sci., Innovation & Tech., *Introducing the AI Safety Institute* (Policy Paper, Nov. 2, 2023); AI Safety Inst., *Advanced AI Evaluations at AISI: May Update* (May 20, 2024); Press Release, U.K. Dept. of Sci., Innovation, and Tech, New Commitment to Deepen Work on Severe AI Risks Concludes AI Seoul Summit (May 22, 2024); Press Release, U.S. Dept. of Comm., U.S. Secretary of Commerce Gina Raimondo Releases Strategic Vision on AI Safety, Announces Plan for Global Cooperation Among AI Safety Institutes (May 21, 2024). Academic experts on artificial intelligence, including two of three computer scientists who received the Turing Award for breakthroughs in the study of deep learning, have expressed similar concerns. *See, e.g.*, Yoshua Bengio et al., *Managing AI Risks in an Era of Rapid Progress*, 384 Science 842 (2024).

[2] Current AI systems do not appear to materially increase risks involving biological weapons development or deployment. *See* Christopher A. Mouton, Caleb Lucas, and Ella Guest, *The Operational Risks of AI in Large-Scale Biological Attacks: A Red-Team Approach*, RAND, RR-A2977-1, 2023. But leading AI developers, including OpenAI, Google DeepMind, and Anthropic, have recognized that future generations of advanced AI may substantially increase such biological risks. *See, e.g.*, Tejal Patwardhan et al., *Building an Early Warning System for LLM-Aided Biological Threat Creation* (2024); Toby Shevlane et al., *Model Evaluation for Extreme Risks*, arXiv (2023); *Oversight of A.I.: Principles for Regulation Before the Subcomm. on Privacy, Tech. and the Law of H. Comm. on the Judiciary*, 118th Cong. (2023) (Written Testimony of Dario Amodei, Ph.D., Co-Founder and CEO, Anthropic). Current models may already exhibit rudimentary versions of the capabilities that could, in future models, give rise to greater biological, chemical, nuclear, and radiological risks. *See, e.g.*, Andres M. Bran et al., *ChemCrow: Augmenting Large-Language Models with Chemistry Tools*, arXiv (2024).

[3] Current AI models exhibit warning signs that future models may possess such capabilities. *See, e.g.*, Richard Fang et al., *LLM Agents Can Autonomously Exploit One-Day Vulnerabilities*, arXiv (2024).

[4] Some of today's most advanced AI systems have already made (much smaller) contributions to malicious phishing campaigns. *See* OpenAI, *Disrupting Malicious Uses of AI by State-Affiliated Threat Actors* (Feb. 11, 2024).

[5] *See* OpenAI, *GPT-4 System Card* 15 (2023) (demonstrating that a prototype version of GPT-4 can deceive third parties, by representing that it is a human, in order to obtain their assistance in solving an online ask); *see also* Jeremy Scheurer et al., *Language Models Can Strategically Deceive Their Users When Put Under Pressure*, arXiv (2023), (demonstrating that AI systems may lie to users and engage in illegal behavior such as insider trading under certain conditions).

databases worldwide, as computer worms have done in the past.[6] If these kinds of serious misuse or malfunctioning occur, they could result in billions of dollars of property damage or mass casualties, through, for example, the damaging of critical financial or health care–related infrastructure.[7]

It is controversial whether any such events *will* occur, how much harm they might cause, and just how large the risks of their occurrence might be. But many leading AI developers and researchers believe that these risks are serious and concerning enough to warrant significant precautionary measures.[8] Developers and policymakers might wish to know, therefore, whether and when developers would be liable to pay compensation for such harm.

This report explores the tort liability of AI developers for large-scale harms to person and property caused by advanced AI systems. Tort law allows parties who suffer injury to sue those who are responsible for injuring them, in order to obtain compensatory damages (and, in certain cases, punitive damages and other remedies). Tort law is principally a form of common law rather than statutory law. That is, tort law is primarily made by courts in the course of adjudicating cases. By contrast, criminal law, the federal copyright laws, and various other bodies of law that establish civil or criminal liability are created by legislatures enacting statutes. While state or federal legislatures might choose to *modify* or *clarify* the tort liability of AI developers, no statutory enactment is required for tort law to apply to AI development (or any other activity); it applies, by default, to activities that foreseeably risk causing harm to person or property.

Our aim in this report is to illuminate the nature and magnitude of AI developers' liability exposure under current U.S. law. Although we focus on large-scale harms, many of the legal doctrines we discuss apply to smaller-scale harms as well. Throughout the discussion, our focus is on developers that initially create (or "train") advanced AI systems, rather than developers who modify them (e.g., through fine-tuning) or augment their capabilities (e.g., through "scaffolding"), or other participants in the AI development process (such as compute providers or chip manufacturers).[9] Our principal aim is to provide a useful picture of the existing legal regime to developers, policymakers, and others who may not have a legal background, although we hope and expect that the discussion will be of use to legal audiences as well. Our discussion is not comprehensive. We do not aim to analyze all the intricacies of applicable legal doctrine, or to assess how judges ought to resolve any uncertainty or unclarity it might contain. Nor do we address the deeper normative, conceptual, and institutional issues about the appropriate scope of tort liability that advanced AI development may raise. Our discussion draws upon a range of sources, including judicial decisions, jury instructions, leading treatises and academic articles, the *Restatement (Second) of Torts*, the *Restatement (Third) of Torts: Liability for Physical and Emotional Harm*, and the *Restatement (Third) of Torts: Products Liability*.

---

[6] Nate Anderson, Confirmed: US and Israel Created Stuxnet, Lost Control of It, Ars Technica blog (June 1, 2012, 6:00 AM), https://arstechnica.com/tech-policy/2012/06/confirmed-us-israel-created-stuxnet-lost-control-of-it/, (describes the propagation of the computer worm StuxNet, which was originally deployed to target Iranian nuclear material refining centrifuges before propagating onto the wider web).

[7] See Daniel M. Gerstein and Erin N. Leidy, *Emerging Technology and Risk Analysis: Artificial Intelligence and Critical Infrastructure*, Homeland Security Operational Analysis Center operated by RAND, RR-A2873-1, 2024, for a discussion of AI's potential applications and dangers to critical infrastructure.

[8] *See, e.g.*, Bengio et al., *supra* note 1.

[9] The "Technical Review" section of the introductory chapter provides an overview of advanced AI systems, AI development, and AI model modification.

We find that AI developers face considerable liability exposure under U.S. tort law for harms caused by their models, particularly if those models are developed or released without utilizing rigorous safety procedures and industry-leading safety practices. That said, tort law's application to AI developers is, in important respects, unclear and uncertain. While liability risk cannot be entirely eliminated, developers can mitigate their exposure by taking rigorous precautions and heightened care in the course of developing, storing, and releasing advanced AI systems.

We identify several key points of potential interest to AI developers, policymakers, lawyers, and standard-setting bodies:

- **Tort law is a significant source of legal risk for developers that do not take adequate precautions to guard against causing harm when developing, storing, testing, or deploying advanced AI systems.** Under existing tort law, there is a general duty to take reasonable care not to cause harm to the person or property of others. This duty applies by default to AI developers—even if targeted liability rules to govern AI development are never enacted by legislatures or regulatory agencies. In Chapter 3, we discuss the requirements of the duty to take reasonable care, and how AI developers might comply (or fail to comply) with these requirements.

- **There is substantial uncertainty, in important respects, about how existing tort doctrine will be applied to AI development. Jurisdictional variation and uncertainty about how legal standards will be interpreted and applied may generate substantial liability risk and costly legal battles for AI developers.** Courts in different states may reach different conclusions on important issues of tort doctrine, especially in novel fact situations. Tort law varies significantly across both domestic and international jurisdictions. In the United States, each state has a different body of tort law, which coexists alongside federal tort law. Which state's tort law applies to a dispute depends on complex choice-of-law rules, which in turn depend on the location of the tortious harm at issue (among other things). Moreover, tort decisions often depend on highly context-specific applications of broad legal standards (such as the negligence standard of "reasonable care") by lay juries. As a result, tort liability can be difficult to predict, particularly with respect to emergent technologies that pose novel legal questions. In the wake of large-scale harms with effects spread across many states, AI developers may face many costly suits across multiple jurisdictions, each with potentially different liability rules. The tort liability incurred by irresponsible AI development may be sufficiently onerous, in the case of sufficiently large-scale damage, to render an AI developer insolvent or force it to declare bankruptcy. Given the cost and risk of litigating a plausible tort suit, moreover, there will often be strong financial incentive for an AI developer (or its liability insurer) to agree to a costly settlement before a verdict is reached.

- **AI developers that do not employ industry-leading safety practices, such as rigorous red-teaming and safety testing or the installation of robust safeguards against misuse, among others,[10] may substantially increase their liability exposure.** Tort law gives significant credit

---

[10] The United Kingdom has identified these techniques, among others, as best practices for managing the risks from advanced AI models and that leading AI companies have already committed to utilizing these practices. U.K. Dept. of Sci., Innovation & Tech., *Emerging Processes for Frontier AI Safety*, 4, 37 (Policy Paper, Oct. 27, 2023).

to industry custom, standards, and practice when determining whether an agent has acted negligently (and is thus liable for the harms it has caused). If most or many industry actors take a certain sort of precaution, this fact will typically be regarded as strong evidence that failing to take this precaution is negligent. Developers who forgo common safety practices in the AI industry, without instituting comparably rigorous safety practices in their stead, may thus increase the likelihood that they will be found negligent should their models cause or enable harm. Therefore, AI developers may wish to consider employing state-of-the-art safety procedures by, for instance, evaluating models for dangerous capabilities, fine-tuning models to limit unsafe behavior, monitoring and moderating models hosted via an application programming interface (API) for dangerous behavior, investing in strong information security measures for model weights, installing reasonably robust safeguards against misuse in potentially dangerous AI systems, and releasing these systems in ways that minimize the chance that third parties will remove the safeguards installed in them.

- **While developers face significant liability exposure from the risk that third parties will misuse their models, there is considerable uncertainty about how this issue will be treated in the courts, and different states may take markedly different approaches.** Most American courts today maintain that a defendant will be liable for negligently enabling a third party to cause harm, maliciously or inadvertently, if this possibility was reasonably foreseeable to the defendant. But "foreseeability" is a pliable concept, and in practice some courts will only hold a defendant liable for enabling third-party misbehavior if such behavior was *readily* or *especially* foreseeable. The risks of misuse of advanced AI systems are being actively discussed and debated, and several leading AI developers take significant precautions to guard against such risks; these facts will tend to support the determination that such misuse was foreseeable, in the event that it occurs. The fact that many of these risks are of a novel kind, and have not previously materialized, may cut in the opposite direction. In some cases, moreover, courts may decline to hold defendants liable for negligently enabling third parties to cause harm even when the possibility of such misuse is foreseeable. For these reasons, and others, there is a good deal of uncertainty about how liability for third-party misuse will be adjudicated in the courts. It would not be surprising if different states took different positions on this issue, just as different states have taken different positions on liability for enabling the misuse of other dangerous instrumentalities (such as guns). Thus, a careless AI developer could face a series of complex and costly legal battles if its model is misused to inflict harm across many jurisdictions.

- **Safety-focused policymakers, developers, and advocates can strengthen AI developers' incentives to employ cutting-edge safety techniques by developing, implementing, and publicizing new safety procedures and by formally promulgating these standards and procedures through industry bodies.** The popularization and proliferation of safe and secure AI development practices by safety-conscious developers and industry bodies can help set industry standards and "customs" that courts may consider when evaluating the liability of other developers, creating stronger incentives for safe and responsible AI development.

- **Policymakers may wish to clarify or modify liability standards for AI developers and/or develop complementary regulatory standards for AI development.** Our analysis suggests that there remains significant uncertainty as to how existing liability law will be applied if harms are caused by advanced AI systems. This uncertainty could conceivably lead some developers to be too cautious, while pushing other developers to neglect the liability risks associated with unsafe development. Clarifying or modifying liability law might thus facilitate responsible innovation and increase the tort system's ability to incentivize safe behavior. Legislation might also help to remedy the inherent limitations of the tort liability system. For example, tort liability cannot easily address the fact that certain AI developers might discount serious risks on the basis of idiosyncratic views, or that an AI company's liability exposure— which is limited by its total assets—might fail to provide it with adequately strong incentives for taking due care. Carefully designed legislation might remedy these shortcomings through the creation of a well-tailored regulatory regime, the clarification or improvement of existing liability law to more clearly identify when a developer or another party is liable for harms, or the establishment of minimum safety requirements for forms of AI development that pose especially significant risks to national security or public welfare.

Contents

Chapter 1

Introduction

Overview

Leading artificial intelligence (AI) developers and researchers, as well as government officials and policymakers, are actively investigating and debating the harms that advanced AI systems might cause, including harms on a large scale.[1] In the future, many developers and researchers believe, advanced AI might be capable of creating (or facilitating the creation of) novel biological and chemical weapons;[2] empowering malicious actors or geopolitical adversaries of the United States to conduct powerful cyberattacks that destabilize critical economic, political, and military infrastructure;[3] and enabling wide-ranging and highly efficient phishing operations or other forms of theft and fraud.[4] In addition to being misused in these or other ways, advanced AI might *malfunction*, by behaving in an undesirable, unexpected, and harmful manner. So, for example, an advanced AI system might attempt to deceive

---

[1] The governments of the United States, the United Kingdom, Australia, Canada, Chile, France, Germany, India, Indonesia, Israel, Italy, Japan, Kenya, Mexico, Netherlands, Nigeria, New Zealand, the Philippines, Republic of Korea, Rwanda, Kingdom of Saudi Arabia, Singapore, Spain, Switzerland, Türkiye, Ukraine, and the European Union have recently expressed concern about—and taken action to address—chemical, biological, radiological, nuclear, cybersecurity-related, and other risks posed by advanced AI systems. See, e.g., Press Release, The White House, President Biden Issues Executive Order on Safe, Secure, and Trustworthy Artificial Intelligence (Oct. 30, 2023); U.K. Dept. of Sci., Innovation & Tech., *Introducing the AI Safety Institute* (Policy Paper, Nov. 2, 2023); AI Safety Inst., *Advanced AI Evaluations at AISI: May Update* (May 20, 2024); Press Release, U.K. Dept. of Sci., Innovation, and Tech, New Commitment to Deepen Work on Severe AI Risks Concludes AI Seoul Summit (May 22, 2024); Press Release, U.S. Dept. of Comm., U.S. Secretary of Commerce Gina Raimondo Releases Strategic Vision on AI Safety, Announces Plan for Global Cooperation Among AI Safety Institutes (May 21, 2024). Academic experts on artificial intelligence, including two of three computer scientists who received the Turing Award for breakthroughs in the study of deep learning, have expressed similar concerns. See, e.g., Yoshua Bengio et al., *Managing AI Risks in an Era of Rapid Progress*, 384 Science 842 (2024).

[2] Current AI systems do not appear to materially increase risks involving biological weapons development or deployment. See Christopher A. Mouton, Caleb Lucas, and Ella Guest, *The Operational Risks of AI in Large-Scale Biological Attacks: A Red-Team Approach*, RAND, RR-A2977-1, 2023. But leading AI developers, including OpenAI, Google DeepMind, and Anthropic, have recognized that future generations of advanced AI may substantially increase such biological risks. See, e.g., Tejal Patwardhan et al., *OpenAI, Building an Early Warning System for LLM-Aided Biological Threat Creation* (2024); Toby Shevlane et al., *Model Evaluation for Extreme Risks*, arXiv (2023); *Oversight of A.I.: Principles for Regulation Before the Subcomm. on Privacy, Tech. and the Law of H. Comm. on the Judiciary*, 118th Cong. (2023) (Written Testimony of Dario Amodei, Ph.D., Co-Founder and CEO, Anthropic). Current models may already exhibit rudimentary versions of the capabilities that could, in future models, give rise to greater biological, chemical, nuclear, and radiological risks. See, e.g., Andres M. Bran et al., *ChemCrow: Augmenting Large-Language Models with Chemistry Tools*, arXiv (2024).

[3] Current AI models exhibit warning signs that future models may possess such capabilities. See, e.g., Richard Fang et al., *LLM Agents Can Autonomously Exploit One-Day Vulnerabilities*, arXiv (2024).

[4] Some of today's most advanced AI systems have already made (much smaller) contributions to malicious phishing campaigns. See OpenAI, *Disrupting Malicious Uses of AI by State-Affiliated Threat Actors* (Feb. 11, 2024).

humans online, without being prompted to do so by its user (or any other party).[5] Certain advanced AI systems might also cause havoc by propagating uncontrollably online, infecting computers and databases worldwide, as computer worms have done in the past.[6] If these kinds of serious misuse or malfunctioning occur, they could result in billions of dollars of property damage or mass casualties, through, for example, the damaging of critical financial or health care–related infrastructure.[7]

It is controversial whether any such events *will* occur, how much harm they might cause, and just how large the risks of their occurrence might be. But many leading AI developers and researchers believe that these risks are serious and concerning enough to warrant significant precautionary measures.[8] Developers and policymakers might wish to know, therefore, whether and when developers would be liable to pay compensation for such harm.

This report explores the tort liability of AI developers, under current U.S. law, for large-scale harms to person and property caused by advanced AI systems. Tort law allows parties who suffer injury to sue those who are responsible for injuring them, in order to obtain compensatory damages (and, in certain cases, punitive damages and other remedies). Tort law is principally a form of common law rather than statutory law; it is primarily made by courts in the course of adjudicating concrete cases. By contrast, criminal law, the federal copyright laws, and various other bodies of law that establish civil or criminal liability are created by legislatures enacting statutes. While state or federal legislatures might choose to *modify* or *clarify* the tort liability of AI developers, no statutory enactment is required for tort law to apply to AI development; it applies, by default, to activities that foreseeably risk causing harm to person or property.

Although we focus on large-scale harms, many of the legal doctrines we discuss apply to smaller-scale harms to person and property as well.[9] Throughout the discussion, our focus is on the tort liability of developers that initially create (or "train") advanced AI systems, rather than parties who modify or augment the capabilities of existing models. Our principal aim is to provide a useful picture of the legal situation to developers, policymakers, and others who may not have a legal background (although we hope and expect that the discussion might be of use to legal audiences as well). Our discussion is not comprehensive. We do not aim to analyze all the intricacies of applicable legal doctrine, or to assess how judges ought to resolve any uncertainty or unclarity it might contain, or to

---

[5] *See* OpenAI, *GPT-4 System Card* 15 (2023) (demonstrating that a prototype version of GPT-4 can deceive third parties, by representing that it is a human, in order to obtain their assistance in solving an online ask); *see also* Jeremy Scheurer et al., *Technical Report: Language Models Can Strategically Deceive Their Users When Put Under Pressure*, arXiv (2023) (demonstrating that AI systems may lie to users and engage in illegal behavior such as insider trading under certain conditions).

[6] Nate Anderson, Confirmed: US and Israel Created Stuxnet, Lost Control of It, Ars Technica blog (June 1, 2012, 6:00 AM), https://arstechnica.com/tech-policy/2012/06/confirmed-us-israel-created-stuxnet-lost-control-of-it/ (describes the propagation of the computer worm StuxNet, which was originally deployed to target Iranian nuclear material refining centrifuges before propagating onto the wider web).

[7] See Daniel M. Gerstein and Erin N. Leidy, *Emerging Technology and Risk Analysis: Artificial Intelligence and Critical Infrastructure*, Homeland Security Operational Analysis Center operated by RAND, RR-A2873-1, 2024, for a discussion of AI's potential applications and dangers to critical infrastructure.

[8] *See, e.g.*, Bengio et al., *supra* note 1.

[9] We do not address tort liability for reputational, emotional, or other forms of injury in this report. Moreover, there are many kinds of harm (such as harms to election security) that the tort system does not redress; these harms fall outside the scope of this report, as well.

address the deeper normative, conceptual, and institutional issues about the appropriate scope of tort liability that advanced AI development may raise.

Methodology

We investigated current tort doctrine in the United States by reviewing leading treatises and academic articles, as well as judicial decisions, jury instructions, the *Restatement (Second) of Torts*, the *Restatement (Third) of Torts: Liability for Physical and Emotional Harm*, and the *Restatement (Third) of Torts: Products Liability*. We identified specific tort doctrines for further analysis based on an assessment of the likelihood that AI-caused harms might implicate those doctrines or that they would otherwise be relevant in potential future litigation on this topic. We accessed these materials through legal research databases, such as Westlaw and LexisNexis, as well as Google Scholar. We conducted research on AI development, its potential harms, and strategies for mitigating these harms by reviewing literature on such databases as arXiv and Google Scholar. In the course of our investigation, we drew upon our prior and contemporaneous experience teaching and researching tort law, related areas of legal doctrine, and the governance of AI.

Organization of This Report

Chapter 2 explains the basic features of tort law and its institutional context. We explore the unpredictability of tort decisions, the complexities that arise in dealing with tort liability exposure across multiple jurisdictions, and the financial ramifications of lost and settled tort suits. In Chapter 3, we turn to the most common tort: negligence. After outlining the structure of the negligence tort and some of its most important features, we elaborate on their implications for the liability risk of AI developers whose models may cause large-scale harm. Then, we briefly examine several further issues—involving intervening agency, causation, and jury decisionmaking—that may play an important role in determining the scope and magnitude of developer liability.

In Chapter 4, we discuss products liability, a specialized form of tort liability, and its potential application to AI models. In Chapter 5, we discuss some forms of strict liability (i.e., liability without any proof of fault) and their potential application to AI developers. In Chapter 6, we discuss the possibility of developer liability under the tort of public nuisance. In Chapter 7, we briefly look at how the First Amendment of the U.S. Constitution and Section 230 of the Communications Decency Act of 1996 may bear on tort liability for AI.

We conclude that AI developers face significant potential liability for harms caused by their models, particularly if those models are developed and deployed without safety precautions commonly employed in the industry. However, there remain significant uncertainties as to how the law will treat these issues. While such risk cannot be entirely eliminated, it can be mitigated by taking rigorous precautions and heightened care when making important decisions about the development, custody, and release of potentially dangerous AI systems.

Technical Review

This section provides a brief overview of advanced AI systems and the processes by which they are developed. Throughout the report, we provide additional explanations of technical concepts and provide citations to appropriate literature in order to help orient readers without relevant technical background.

The report's analysis is relevant to both existing and future AI systems. An AI system is, very roughly speaking, a system that utilizes algorithms and statistical models derived from machine learning methods in order to generate content, accomplish tasks, and make predictions about novel data and situations. *Narrow* AI systems are designed to perform domain-specific tasks. Some narrow AI systems may pose significant risks of large-scale harm.[10] Such risks may also be posed by AI systems that are built on or incorporate *foundation models*. Foundation models are trained on large and diverse datasets (such as text corpora scraped from large portions of the internet). Recent AI systems built on foundation models, such as OpenAI's GPT-4, Anthropic's Claude 3, Google's Gemini, and Meta's Llama 3, "exhibit high performance across a broad domain of cognitive tasks, often performing the tasks as well as, or better than, a human."[11] These domains include computer vision, software coding, and natural language processing.[12] Many AI systems that have been the focus of recent public attention, including AI chatbots such as ChatGPT (which is built on GPT-3.5 and GPT-4), incorporate or are built on foundation models.

Foundation models can be modified to perform well at particular tasks through a process known as "fine-tuning," which modifies a model's weights. Model weights are "numerical values used to specify how the input (e.g., text describing an image) is transformed into the output (e.g., the image itself). These are iteratively updated during model training to improve the model's performance on the tasks for which it is trained."[13] During fine-tuning, model developers take an existing foundation model and train it on a specific task, such as responding to written instructions or summarizing financial documents, in order to adapt the model's learned features and parameters to perform well on that particular task.[14] Narrow models can, like foundation models, be fine-tuned in order to enhance their ability to perform their intended functions.

Of particular relevance for our analysis, AI models can also be fine-tuned in order to *prevent* them from exercising dangerous or risky capabilities. In other words, developers can install "safeguards" in AI models by fine-tuning them so as to prevent or reduce unwanted model behaviors, such as providing private information, writing code to execute a cyberattack, using racist epithets, or providing

---

[10] Biological design tools, which may facilitate the creation of novel biological agents, are a notable example. While such tools have beneficial uses, they may also pose risks of large-scale harm. *See generally* Jonas B. Sandbrink, *Artificial Intelligence and Biological Misuse: Differentiating Risks of Language Models and Biological Design Tools*, arXiv (2023).

[11] Elizabeth Seger et al., *Open-Sourcing Highly Capable Foundation Models: An Evaluation of Risks, Benefits, and Alternative Methods for Pursuing Open-Source Objectives*, arXiv 6 (2023).

[12] *See* Rishi Bommasani et al., *On the Opportunities and Risks of Foundation Models*, arXiv (2022).

[13] Seger et al., *supra* note 11, at 9.

[14] *See* Jacobin Devlin et al., *BERT: Pre-Training of Deep Bidirectional Transformers for Language Understanding*, arXiv (2019).

targeted instructions on how to create biological and chemical weapons.[15] Conversely, it is possible to use fine-tuning in order to *remove* these safeguards, thereby gaining access to the model's dangerous capabilities, or to use fine-tuning to *augment* the model's dangerous capabilities. Recent research suggests that removing safeguards through fine-tuning will often be a comparatively easy and straightforward task.[16]

The public accessibility of AI models is also relevant for any analysis of liability risk and the risks of damage from AI systems. We consider two general forms of releasing AI models to the public: *open-sourcing* and *closed-sourcing*.[17]

Open-sourcing AI models is, roughly speaking, the practice of making key model components publicly available for download, thereby allowing third-party actors to re-create, modify, and use the AI model. These components may include the model's weights (the mathematical function that takes in the model's inputs and produces its outputs), the model's architecture (which specifies the high-level structure of the model), its training code (which executes algorithms used to update the model weights during training), and its inference code (which actively runs the model, once it is trained, using its weights and architecture).[18] We use "open-source models" to refer to models for which *at least* model weights and model architecture are publicly accessible—with access to these two components, most downstream developers can easily write inference code to reproduce and run the model.[19] At least at present, open-sourcing enables third parties to remove any safeguards against misuse that a developer has installed in its model. For it is fairly easy (and inexpensive) to "fine-tune" an open-source model so as to remove these safeguards against misuse—thereby enabling the model to perform various additional tasks, including potentially dangerous or injurious ones.[20] There are active research programs aimed at mitigating this problem, so it is possible that open-source developers will be able to install more robust safeguards against misuse in the future.[21]

Closed-sourcing AI models is, roughly speaking, the practice of providing public access to models in ways that do not permit users to download those model components that would allow users to easily reproduce the model. A closed-source AI developer typically provides access to its models through a structured user interface, such as an application programming interface (API) or web user interface, which it controls. This enables closed-source developers to exercise some degree of control over how their AI models are used.[22] Such a developer can, for instance, curtail the ability of users to

---

[15] *See, e.g.,* OpenAI, *supra* note 5, at 3, 13 (discussing OpenAI's fine-tuning of GPT-4 to refuse requests for personal information or "illicit advice"); Gemini Team, Google, *Gemini: A Family of Highly Capable Multimodal Models*, arXiv 29 (2023) (discussing the fine-tuning of Gemini to generate "harmless" responses). Anthropic uses a similar process to prevent harmful model behaviors. Anthropic, *The Claude 3 Model Family: Opus, Sonnet, Haiku* 3 (2024).

[16] *See, e.g.,* Pranav Gade et al., *BadLlama: Cheaply Removing Safety Fine-Tuning from Llama 2-Chat 13B*, arXiv (2023).

[17] For a more detailed discussion of the various forms of open-source and closed-source release, see Irene Solaiman, *The Gradient of Generative AI Release: Methods and Considerations*, arXiv (2023); and Seger et al., *supra* note 11.

[18] Seger et al., *supra* note 11, at 9.

[19] *Id.* at 10.

[20] *Id.* at 12. *See generally* Gade et al., *supra* note 16.

[21] *See, e.g.,* Peter Henderson et al., *Self-Destructing Models: Increasing the Costs of Harmful Dual Uses of Foundation Models*, arXiv (2022); Jiangyi Deng et al., *SOPHON: Non-Fine-Tunable Learning to Restrain Task Transferability for Pre-Trained Models*, arXiv (2024).

[22] *See* Toby Shevlane, *Structured Access: An Emerging Paradigm for Safe AI Deployment*, arXiv 1 (2022).

fine-tune its models, and thereby curtail their ability to remove or circumvent the model's safeguards.[23] At present, however, the degree of control that closed-source developers can exercise over such attempts is limited.[24] As in the case of open-source models, it is possible that research progress in AI safety will mitigate this problem in the future.

---

[23] Closed-source developers can also provide researchers and other parties with the ability to inspect, fine-tune, or modify model weights without giving such researchers full access to the model or copies of the model. *See* Benjamin S. Bucknall & Robert F. Trager, *Structured Access for Third-Party Safety Research on Frontier AI Models Investigating Researchers' Model Access Requirements* (GovAI and Oxford Martin Sch. Working Paper, 2023).

[24] *See, e.g.*, Kellin Perline et al., *Exploiting Novel GPT-4 APIs*, arXiv (2023); Qiusi Zhan et al., *Removing RLHF Protections in GPT-4 via Fine-Tuning*, arXiv (2024).

Chapter 2

The Nature of Tort Law

In this chapter, we explain the basic nature of tort law and lay out some basic tort principles that will govern the determination of liability for damages caused by advanced AI systems. In particular, we highlight that tort law is a form of common law, which is primarily developed in the courts by judges through the accumulation of decisions about particular cases. We discuss how tort law is elaborated, modified, and applied by judges and juries; the significance of the fact that different states have independent bodies of tort law; the various remedies that tort law provides for wrongful injury; and the significance of the fact that jury decisionmaking is highly discretionary and unstructured, as well as the fact that the large majority of tort cases settle before or during trial. These basics lay the foundation for a deeper discussion of specific tort doctrines in future chapters.

Tort Law Is Common Law

Tort law is primarily a form of common law.[25] Common law is made through, and reported in, judicial decisions about litigated cases, rather than statutes passed by legislatures or regulations passed by administrative agencies.[26] While tort law has largely developed in an incremental and piecemeal fashion, judges have occasionally made sweeping and rapid changes to it.[27] Many landmark tort decisions have arisen from cases on appeal to the highest court in the relevant jurisdiction (such as the New York Court of Appeals or the Supreme Court of California). In these final courts of appeal, and in lower courts, judges sometimes expand or narrow rules drawn from applicable precedents in order to address novel circumstances or avoid a result that seems manifestly impractical or unjust. Sometimes, judges will flatly overrule applicable precedents in order to keep the law in step with evolving societal circumstances or sensibilities.[28]

---

[25] Cong. Rsch. Serv., *Introduction to Tort Law* (IF11291, 2023) ("Tort law has also historically been a matter of common law rather than statutory law; that is, judges (not legislatures) developed many of tort law's fundamental principles through case-by-case adjudication."). *See also Tort, Black's Law Dictionary* (11th ed. 2019) (defining torts).

[26] *See Common Law, Black's Law Dictionary* (11th ed. 2019). While tort is mostly a body of judge-made law, tort liability has been imposed or modified by statute in certain circumstances, and statutory enactments are often quite relevant to determining tort liability. A defendant's breach of a statutory duty, for instance, may be powerful or even conclusive proof that it has acted negligently. *Restatement (Third) of Torts: Phys. & Emot. Harm* § 14 (2010). See also Mark Geistfeld, *Tort Law in the Age of Statutes*, 99 Iowa L. Rev. 957 (2013), for a broader discussion of the relationship between the common-law tort system and legislative statutes.

[27] David G. Owen, *Design Defect Ghosts*, 74 Brook L. Rev. 927, 935 (2009) (characterizing the birth of strict products liability in the twentieth century as a "a rapid, widespread, and altogether explosive change in the rules and theory of legal responsibility").

[28] Some of the most famous cases in the American tort law canon, such as Judge Benjamin Cardozo's opinion in *MacPherson v. Buick Motor Co.*, repudiated reasonably robust lines of existing precedent. *See MacPherson v. Buick Motor Co.*, 217 N.Y. 382, 384, 111 N.E. 1050 (1916).

In determining how legal issues in tort cases ought to be resolved, judges look to applicable precedents, and sometimes these precedents clearly favor the plaintiff or the defendant. But much of tort law consists of broad and open-textured standards. Many of these standards, moreover, are applied by lay juries. For instance, once a plaintiff's claim has survived summary judgment (i.e., the judge has submitted the case to the jury because she has found that the plaintiff has put forward plausible factual claims that, if true, would ground a legal claim to redress), the jury must decide (among other things) whether the defendant failed to take reasonable care—often the most important question in a case.[29] In answering such questions, "the jury has a great deal of normative discretion."[30] Indeed, the jury probably has more power in negligence cases (which form the bulk of tort cases) than it has in any other common-law area.[31] Thus, the determination of tort liability is often highly contextual, fact-sensitive, and difficult to predict. For this reason, both parties often face a significant risk of receiving an adverse result if they litigate a case to final judgment. These factors help to explain why the vast majority of tort claims are settled before or during trial. Agreeing to a settlement allows both parties to avoid the onerousness and expense of trial and the substantial risk of receiving an adverse judgment.[32]

Tort Law Varies Considerably Across Jurisdictions, Including Those Within the United States

Tort law is jurisdictionally specific. Tort rules are made by judges within specific jurisdictions, and the precedent that a judge creates through one ruling is only binding on future cases within that same jurisdiction.[33] For this reason, specific tort rules often vary considerably from one common-law jurisdiction to another. Unsurprisingly, there is even *more* variation between jurisdictions in the United States and jurisdictions in other countries. In some jurisdictions, such as France, tort law has features—such as a default rule of strict liability for harm caused by dangerous instrumentalities under the defendant's control—that pose heightened legal risks for AI developers.[34] Given the global nature of many large-scale harms, a complete analysis of liability exposure for such harms would need to engage with all relevant jurisdictions, a formidable task that is well beyond the scope of this report. For now, it suffices to say that an AI developer that makes its model widely available in the United States or the rest of the world may find itself subject to a wide variety of liability rules for harms caused in

---

[29] *Restatement (Third) of Torts: Phys. & Emot. Harm* § 8 (2010).

[30] Mark P. Gergen, *The Jury's Role in Deciding Normative Issues in the American Common Law*, 68 Fordham L. Rev. 407, 425 (1999).

[31] *Id.* at 424.

[32] *See* Samuel R. Gross & Kent D. Syverud, *Don't Try: Civil Jury Verdicts in a System Geared to Settlement*, 44 UCLA L. Rev. 1 (1996) (discussing how the civil justice system is geared toward encouraging settlement); Matt Galanter, *The Vanishing Trial: An Examination of Trials and Related Matters in Federal and State Courts*, 1 J. of Empirical Legal Stud. 459 (2004) (discussing that trials have declined about 60 percent since the mid-1980s, and that tort trials in particular have declined).

[33] *Precedent, Black's Law Dictionary* (11th ed. 2019). A jury verdict, by contrast, is usually limited to the individual case.

[34] For a discussion of French tort law, see Eva Steiner, *French Law: A Comparative Approach* (2d ed. 2018), 250–80. For further discussion of strict liability in the United States, see Chapter 5.

different jurisdictions. A single action that causes harm in multiple jurisdictions may escape liability altogether in some jurisdictions while incurring onerous liability in others.

In the United States, tort liability is almost entirely a creature of state law. Strictly speaking, most of the time there is no such thing as "U.S. tort law"; instead, there is California tort law, New York tort law, New Jersey tort law, and so on. There are also narrow enclaves of federal tort (or tort-like) law, such as liability for harms under admiralty law, which governs cases that arise on maritime waters.[35] Federal courts do hear disputes arising under these narrow enclaves of federal tort law, but they also adjudicate disputes between citizens of different states, and, when doing so, they apply state tort law. More generally, state tort law governs the vast majority of tortious harms, including the potential tortious harms that AI might cause.[36] Complex choice-of-law rules determine which body (or bodies) of state and federal law will govern a given dispute.[37]

There is considerable variation among the various bodies of state tort law, including on some very important issues. For example, New York takes a very different position from California on the liability of product manufacturers for harms caused by third parties who have altered and misused the manufacturers' products. In New York, it is quite difficult for an injured plaintiff to recover against such a manufacturer, whereas in California (and most other states) such a manufacturer may be held liable so long as the alteration that caused injury was reasonably foreseeable.[38] Despite this jurisdictional variation, there is also a great deal of overlap between the tort laws of the several states. The American Law Institute (a private, nonprofit entity composed of judges, lawyers, and legal academics) attempts to synthesize and elucidate the common elements in these different states' bodies of common law (including their bodies of tort law) by issuing *Restatements of the Law*.[39] The American Law Institute is the primary body in the United States that attempts to synthesize the different states' bodies of common law. Judges and scholars often treat these *Restatements* as highly persuasive, and state courts will often "adopt" doctrinal rules from them. This report will, accordingly, draw substantially from relevant *Restatements* as well. *Restatements* help to maintain a degree of consistency and uniformity across the various bodies of state tort law. It is worth emphasizing, however, that state courts are not automatically bound by *Restatements* and often depart from them in significant respects. There are sometimes large conflicts between the positions taken by earlier and later *Restatements* of a given body of law, and courts sometimes continue to align themselves with an earlier *Restatement* rather than repudiating it in favor of its successor. Moreover, state courts generally do not adopt a

---

[35] *See* Cong. Rsch. Serv., *Federal Admiralty and Maritime Jurisdiction Part 4: Torts and Maritime Contracts or Services* (LSB10827, 2022).

[36] *See, e.g., Erie Railroad Co. v. Tompkins*, 304 U.S. 64 (1938) (holding that federal courts should apply state "substantive law" when deciding claims brought under state law). Tort law is generally considered substantive, and hence federal courts apply it when hearing state tort claims in federal court.

[37] *See generally* Symeon Symeonides, *Choice of Law* (2016), esp. chap. 8.

[38] *Compare Robinson v. Reed-Prentice Div. of Package Mach. Co.*, 403 N.E.2d 440 (N.Y. 1980) ("We hold that a manufacturer of a product may not be cast in damages, either on a strict products liability or negligence cause of action, where, after the product leaves the possession and control of the manufacturer, there is a subsequent modification which substantially alters the product and is the proximate cause of plaintiff's injuries.") *with* CACI No. 1245. Affirmative Defense—Product Misuse or Modification (California jury instructions stating that a product's modification or misuse should provide its manufacturer with a complete defense against liability only where the manufacturer can prove that "it was so highly extraordinary it was not reasonably foreseeable").

[39] Legal Information Institute, *Restatement of the Law* (Aug. 2020).

Restatement wholesale; they tend to adopt *Restatement* provisions in a more selective and piecemeal fashion. For these reasons, among others, there is considerable variation between different states' bodies of tort law, notwithstanding the influence of the *Restatements*.

An important difference among state court systems is that some of them tend to be more sympathetic to plaintiffs than others.[40] Similarly, the state and federal court systems may afford quite different prospects to a litigant for multiple reasons, including differences in applicable evidentiary and procedural rules. This is why the parties to a tort suit often care a great deal about whether the dispute will be heard in state court or "removed" to a federal court: Even if it is clear which body of substantive law will govern the dispute, the odds of victory or defeat may depend substantially on the forum in which the dispute is heard.

As a result of this jurisdictional variation, it is often difficult to determine the specific outcome of a hypothetical tort case, particularly for large-scale harms. The outcome will be determined by the specific state or federal body of law that governs the case. Large-scale harms may affect people in multiple or even most U.S. states, giving rise to causes of action under many different bodies of tort law. The fact that some states' tort laws and courts are considerably more plaintiff-friendly than others' increases the chance that an AI developer will incur *some* substantial amount of tort liability in *some* district if a model or system it releases is demonstrably the cause of large-scale physical harm or property damage.

Sophisticated commercial firms often purchase a considerable amount of liability insurance in order to protect themselves against the risks of civil suits (in tort law and more generally).[41] Liability insurers generally take the lead in defending firms against tort suits and deciding whether to settle them. It is liability insurers that typically pay most of the costs of tort suits and adverse tort judgments. After a tort suit, however, some of these costs will be passed on to defendants in the form of higher premiums. It will often be in the rational self-interest of a defendant firm and its liability insurer to settle a tort suit, at considerable cost, rather than continue litigation and risk incurring the full financial burden of an adverse judgment. For this reason, the legal "gray areas" of tort law may generate significant financial burdens for firms defending against plausible tort suits by rationally incentivizing them (or their liability insurers) to strike costly settlement agreements with plaintiffs. This will often be true even if those gray areas would plausibly be resolved in favor of the defendants if the cases were litigated to final judgment. Therefore, even if the law does not clearly deem an AI developer liable for a certain sort of harm, it will often be in a developer's rational self-interest to take significant precautionary measures against causing that sort of harm, in order to reduce the likelihood of tort suits that could result in significant financial and reputational costs.

It is also worth observing, however, that the role of liability insurers is often dramatically reduced in the context of *mass tort* suits—that is, suits involving a very large number of claims arising out of the same harmful activity or incident. Mass tort defendants typically retain control over their own defense,

---

[40] Finding the most sympathetic venue for a case is often referred to as *forum shopping* and is a major strategic focus for litigators. *See Forum-Shopping*, Black's Law Dictionary (11th ed. 2019). *See also* Richard Maloy, *Forum Shopping? What's Wrong with That?*, 24 QLR 25, 26–33 (2005) (discusses the definition and history of forum shopping in the United States).

[41] On liability insurance and its bearing on tort law and doctrine, see Tom Baker, *Liability Insurance as Tort Regulation: Six Ways That Liability Insurance Shapes Tort Law in Action*, 12 Conn. Ins. L.J. 1 (2005); Kenneth S. Abraham & Catherine M. Sharkey, *The Glaring Gap in Tort Theory*, 133 Yale L.J. 2165 (2024); Mark Geistfeld, *Legal Ambiguity, Liability Insurance, and Tort Reform*, 60 DePaul L. Rev. 539 (2011).

and they typically use their own funds to settle claims, obtaining indemnification from liability insurers later, if at all.[42] This is the case for multiple reasons, including the fact that "some defendants have no true risk-transfer liability insurance at all, or they may have liability insurance that expressly excludes the mass tort liabilities in question."[43] The sorts of large-scale harms under consideration from AI may give rise to mass tort suits; and it will sometimes be highly difficult, or even impossible, to obtain liability insurance for many such large-scale harms, in light of their highly correlated nature.[44]

The fact that defendant firms often lack the liability insurance to cover their mass tort exposure helps to explain why mass tort suits not infrequently render defendants insolvent or force them to declare bankruptcy.[45] In addition, tort suits regarding large-scale or otherwise highly salient harms from AI are likely to generate significant public attention, which may impose large reputational costs, as well as financial costs, on the defendant developer.

Remedies for Torts: Compensatory Damages, Punitive Damages, and Injunctions

Virtually all tort suits occur after a defendant's wrongful or risky activity has caused the plaintiff to suffer harm. These suits seek *compensatory damages*, which aim to restore the plaintiff—insofar as possible—to the position she would have been in had she not suffered the harm in question.[46] A plaintiff can typically recover damages for *physical harms*—that is, bodily injury or damage to real or tangible property. These damages compensate the plaintiff for any economic or emotional harm she has suffered as a consequence of the physical harm in question (such as the lost wages and loss of life's pleasures caused by a physically disabling injury). Actions that cause severe injuries or death, extensive damage to property or infrastructure, or injury to wealthy plaintiffs may thus force the defendant to pay a considerable sum in damages.

A defendant who has acted in an especially culpable or egregious manner may also be liable to pay the plaintiff *punitive damages*. An award of punitive damages can be much higher than the underlying award of compensatory damages in the same case. In setting such an award, juries may take into account the defendant's wealth and the extent to which the defendant's conduct can be fairly characterized as egregious or outrageous.[47] Relatively few successful tort plaintiffs obtain punitive damages; such damages were awarded in only 5 percent of state tort cases, according to one study.[48] Nevertheless, the possibility of an onerous punitive damages award may have a significant effect on

---

[42] Baker, *supra* note 41, at 1572.

[43] *Id.* at 1584.

[44] See generally Kenneth S. Abraham & Daniel Schwarcz, *Courting Disaster: The Underappreciated Risk of a Cyber-Insurance Catastrophe*, 27 Conn. Ins. L.J. 407 (2021).

[45] On mass torts in bankruptcy, see generally Anthony J. Casey & Joshua C. Macey, *In Defense of Chapter 11 for Mass Torts*, 90 U. Chi. L. Rev. 973 (2023).

[46] *Restatement (Second) of Torts* § 903 (1979).

[47] *Id.* § 908 (1979).

[48] U.S. Dept. of Just., *Punitive Damage Awards in State Courts, 2005* (2011).

rationally self-interested corporate behavior and enhance defendants' incentives to settle rather than litigate tort suits.[49]

In some cases, a plaintiff is able to obtain judicial relief against a defendant's demonstrably tortious behavior *before* the behavior has caused the plaintiff to suffer harm. In such a case, the court will issue a *permanent injunction*, also called a *final injunction*, which is an order to undertake or refrain from undertaking certain actions, so as to avoid causing tortious injuries.[50] Despite its name, the permanent injunction need not be permanent. Rather, it is *indefinite*: It may be lifted or modified by a court in light of changed circumstances, but until and unless that happens, it remains in force.[51] Courts may outline conditions under which they will lift an injunction, but the content of those conditions and the determination that they have been met are decisions usually left to the discretion of the court.

To obtain a permanent injunction, the plaintiff must establish that the defendant is likely to act in a way that would be tortious. Whether an injunction is available will then depend on a complex balancing test, which turns on such factors as the magnitude and seriousness of harm the plaintiff might suffer if the injunction is not granted; the adequacy of the remedies that will be available to the plaintiff after they suffer this harm; the cost to the defendant of complying with the proposed injunction, should it turn out to be unnecessary, premature, or otherwise inappropriate; and the likelihood that the plaintiff will suffer harm if the injunction is not granted.[52]

Importantly, a plaintiff does not need to show that they are *likely* to suffer harm unless the injunction is granted. Even establishing a comparatively small probability of harm may suffice for an injunction if the magnitude of this harm is sufficiently large: "How great a threat is sufficient, or how great a probability is dangerous, depends on all the factual circumstances in the case."[53] This "balancing of interests cannot be avoided, and it cannot be reduced to preponderance of the evidence or any other attempt to specify a level of probability."[54]

There exists, therefore, the possibility that a court could grant an injunction against a firm on the basis that the firm's continued development or future release of a highly capable AI system poses a serious risk of catastrophic harm. In practice, many courts may be inclined to dismiss such requests for injunctive relief as resting on unduly speculative or contestable empirical assumptions. Courts will be more likely to entertain such requests, however, if similar AI systems have already caused other large-scale harms or caused small-scale harms that credibly demonstrate the ability to cause harm on a much larger scale.

While injunctive relief is an important tool for courts to regulate dangerous behavior, most court cases are brought after harms have occurred. It is often difficult, after all, for a plaintiff to discern that a defendant has subjected her to a risk of harm until it has actually materialized. Suits for

---

[49] *See* Thomas Koenig, *The Shadow Effect of Punitive Damages on Settlements*, Wis. L. Rev. 169 (1998).

[50] *Restatement (Third) of Torts: Remedies (Tentative Draft No. 2)* § 43 (2023). In contrast to a "preliminary injunction," by which one party in a law trial can seek to temporarily halt the other party's behavior—pending the result of the trial—obtaining a permanent injunction against a defendant's tortious behavior is the plaintiff's *goal* (or one of their goals) in a tort suit.

[51] *Restatement (Third) of Remedies (Tentative Draft No. 2)* § 43 cmt. c, at 465 (2023).

[52] *Restatement (First) of Torts* §§ 933, 936 (1939); *Restatement (Third) of Remedies (Tentative Draft No. 2)* § 43 (2023).

[53] *Restatement (Third) of Remedies (Tentative Draft No. 2)* § 46 cmt. g (2023).

[54] *Id.* § 46 cmt g., rep.'s note.

compensatory damages, brought once harm has been inflicted, are far more common and will be the focus of the next chapter of this report.

Chapter 3

Negligence

Most tort cases are negligence cases. How the law of negligence will apply to AI development is, therefore, particularly important for developers and policymakers to understand.[55] The law of negligence is rooted in the idea that actors have an obligation to exercise reasonable caution in order to avoid causing foreseeable injury to other people's bodies or property.[56] When actors fail to take reasonable care in a given set of circumstances, they can be held liable for the harms their actions cause.

In this chapter, we begin by laying out the basic structure of the American law of negligence. We then consider how negligence doctrine is likely to apply to AI developers should their products cause harm. Negligence doctrine is a vast terrain, and so our discussion is far from comprehensive. We attempt to address some doctrinal issues of special importance to AI developers to help developers understand when they might be held liable for the third-party misuse of its model. We also address the potential difficulties that an injured plaintiff may face in demonstrating that a developer's negligence was the cause of an injury.

Our most important finding is the importance of industry standards and practices in the law of negligence as it may be applied to AI. In determining whether a developer has been negligent, courts will likely be strongly influenced by industry standards and best practices regarding AI safety. Developers that employ such standards and safety practices are less likely to be found negligent should their models cause harm.

The Structure of Negligence Law and Its Application to AI Development

To bring a successful negligence claim, an injured plaintiff must establish (by a preponderance of the evidence) each of the following elements:

- **Duty:** The defendant (D) owed the plaintiff (P) a *duty of care*. In general, each actor has a duty to take reasonable care against causing foreseeable harm to other people's bodies and property. The duty to take reasonable care against causing harm to person or property is a fairly expansive one, which many courts limit only in "exceptional cases, when an articulated countervailing principle or policy warrants denying or limiting liability in a particular class of cases."[57] By contrast, there is no duty to take care—except in fairly limited circumstances—

---

[55] *See* Kenneth S. Abraham, *Forms and Functions of Tort Law* 52 (5th ed. 2017).

[56] *Restatement (First) of Torts* § 282 (1934).

[57] *Restatement (Third) of Torts* § 7 (2010).

14

against causing other people pure economic loss (i.e., intangible monetary injuries, such as lost profits) or stand-alone emotional harms (i.e., those not stemming from a bodily injury).[58] Typically, however, a plaintiff who recovers for damage to her body or property can *also* recover for economic or emotional harm he suffers in consequence.

- **Breach:** D *breached* their duty of care by acting without sufficient care, such as by taking inadequate precautions or unleashing an unreasonably high risk. In determining whether the defendant breached its duty of care, courts often ask how much care, or what forms of precaution, a "reasonably prudent person" in the defendant's position would have used.[59] Sometimes, courts ask whether the risks imposed by that the defendant's action were justified by its social utility.

- **Factual causation:** D's action was the *factual cause* of P's injury. Typically, this means that if D had not acted in a tortious manner, P would not have suffered the injury in question. In certain cases, however, this "but-for" test of factual causation seems to get the wrong result; in such cases, courts may use a different test.[60] (For example, if D shoots and paralyzes P, P can recover against D even if it can be demonstrated that some other wrongdoer would have shot and paralyzed P shortly thereafter.)

- **Proximate cause:** D's action was the *proximate cause* of P's injury. Proximate-cause doctrine typically limits a negligent defendant's liability to *foreseeable* harms, and to the sorts of harms that made his or her action negligent in the first place.[61] Courts may also use proximate-cause doctrine to avoid consequences they regard as undesirable from a policy perspective.[62]

It is for the judge to decide whether the defendant owed the plaintiff a duty of care. As previously mentioned, the duty to take care against causing foreseeable harm to others' persons or property is an expansive one—most states hold that the duty of care is owed, by default, to everyone whose person or property a defendant's action foreseeably puts at risk. Accordingly, the *Restatement (Third)* says, limitations on the duty of care are "exceptional" in cases involving physical injury or property

---

[58] Thus, if P's business loses profits because D has carelessly destroyed someone else's property, P will typically be unable to recover damages for their loss. (If D has caused P's business to lose profits by carelessly destroying *their* property, P will be able to recover for this loss because it is "consequential" or "parasitic" on the tort that D committed against their property rights.) That said, plaintiffs are sometimes able to circumvent the negligence tort's bar on recovery for pure economic loss by bringing a claim in public nuisance—a tort that is somewhat obscure but increasingly important. *See* Catherine M. Sharkey, *Public Nuisance as Modern Business Tort: A New Unified Framework for Liability for Economic Harms*, 70 DePaul L. Rev. 431 (2020). While a discussion of public nuisance is beyond the scope of this memo, it is worth noting that if an AI developer is held liable for the pure economic loss caused by (the use of) its model, this could massively increase the extent of its liability. It is also worth noting that other legal systems are far more liberal in allowing tort recovery for pure economic loss. *See generally Pure Economic Loss in Europe* (Mauro Bussani & Vernon Valentine Palmer, eds., 2003).

[59] *See Restatement (Third) of Torts: Phys. & Emot. Harm* § 3 cmt. a (2010) (noting that a person is negligent, and therefore breaches their duty of care, when they fail to act as a "reasonably prudent person").

[60] *Restatement (Third) of Torts: Phys. & Emot. Harm* § 27 (2010).

[61] For example, suppose that D negligently crashes into P's car, forcing P to walk home while his car is towed away. If P is struck by lightning as he is walking home, courts are unlikely to hold D liable for this injury, although P would not have suffered it if D had not acted negligently.

[62] *Restatement (Third) of Torts: Phys. & Emot. Harm* § 6 spec. note (2010).

damage.[63] However, a judge may find that the defendant did not owe the plaintiff a duty of care for several reasons. First, a judge will sometimes find that the plaintiff was an unforeseeable victim of the defendant's conduct. Since the concept of "foreseeability" is a pliable one, the role that foreseeability plays in duty analysis creates a significant degree of judicial discretion to deny that the defendant was under any duty of care to the defendant—a conclusion that will keep the case from getting to a jury.[64] Second, a judge may decline to find a duty of care in certain cases on the basis of one or more compelling public policy considerations—such as, for example, the fact that the defendant is a public utility that provides important public services (which would be adversely affected by its insolvency), or the possibility that recognizing a duty of care in the case at hand would expose the defendant (or other defendants similarly situated) to "enormous" liability.[65] The role of public policy considerations in determining duty again injects considerable uncertainty into any attempt to predict how a judge might rule in factually novel circumstances. For example, while the threat of "enormous" liability has produced "no duty" rulings in certain kinds of cases, there are other kinds of cases—such as litigation involving asbestos and other toxic substances—in which a duty of care *has* been recognized, enormous liability notwithstanding, thus opening the door to very large settlements or damage awards.[66]

If the judge decides that the defendant *did* owe the plaintiff a duty of care, the jury must then decide whether the defendant has breached this duty, and whether the other elements of the negligence cause of action (injury, factual causation, proximate causation) are satisfied as well. The judge is empowered to take these issues away from the jury, however, and rule on them "as a matter of law," if she determines that a reasonable jury could only rule in one way.[67]

Much of the action in a negligence suit revolves around the jury's determination as to whether the defendant breached its duty of care: Given the risks, were the defendant's decisions or course of conduct reasonable? In making this breach determination, juries often ask whether a reasonably prudent person in the defendant's position would have acted as the defendant did. This "reasonable person" standard is objective rather than subjective; even if the actual defendant had good intentions, failed to consider relevant risks, or assigned low probability to the risks, the jury will evaluate the reasonableness of the defendant's actions against the jury's assessment of the risks a reasonable person would have accounted for given the available evidence. In the case of AI harms, these risks may include those that other industry experts have highlighted publicly or privately.[68] *Awareness* of the relevant risks is not necessary to establish breach; the question is whether the defendant *should* have been aware

---

[63] *Restatement (Third) of Torts: Phys. & Emot. Harm* § 7 (2010) (discussing the rules surrounding duty and the certain circumstances where the duty of care may be limited).

[64] W. Jonathan Cardi, *Purging Foreseeability: The New Vision and Judicial Power in the Proposed Restatement (Third) of Torts*, 58 Vand. L. Rev. 739, 740 (2005) ("[B]ecause duty is the sole element of negligence not left in the first instance to the jury, duty—and hence foreseeability—has become the primary source of judicial power to weed out cases deemed by a judge to be unworthy.").

[65] *Strauss v. Belle Realty Co.*, 482 N.E.2d 34, 36 (N.Y. 1985) (citing *Prosser and Keeton on the Law of Torts* § 92, at 663 (W. Page Keeton, ed., 5th ed. 1984)).

[66] See Paul D. Carrington, *The Consequences of Asbestos Litigation*, 26 Rev. Litig. 740 (2007), for an overview of the size and scale of damages assessed in asbestos cases.

[67] *Restatement (Third) of Torts: Phys. & Emot. Harm* § 8 (2010).

[68] For risks that have already been highlighted publicly, see *supra* note 2.

of them. At the same time, the fact that a defendant *was* aware of serious safety risks entailed by its actions may strongly support a finding of breach.[69]

In some cases, particularly those involving products, juries may ask whether the risks of the defendant's action (e.g., releasing a possibly dangerous product into the market) outweighed its social utility.[70] Economic analysts of tort law often model the jury's determination of breach as a cost-benefit balancing test, which weighs the expected costs of the defendant's action against its expected benefits in order to determine whether the action was negligent.[71] In practice, however, juries probably determine breach in a less rigorous, more impressionistic way than these economic models might suggest. In particular, there is strong evidence that "lay individuals, jurors, and judges elevate safety considerations over monetary cost in a manner that is inconsistent with cost-benefit analysis."[72] Jury instructions typically provide the jury with great latitude to determine what reasonable care requires; they do not prescribe engaging in cost-benefit analysis or any other method of decisionmaking.[73]

Finally, negligence law accords great significance to industry custom and standards, where applicable.[74] If the defendant's action complied with safety standards that are widely accepted in the industry, this will generally be treated as powerful (albeit not dispositive) evidence that the defendant was not negligent.[75] By the same token, if the defendant's action *did not* comply with widely accepted safety standards, this will generally be treated as powerful (albeit not dispositive) evidence that the defendant's action *was* negligent. The relevant safety standards can be informal—that is, developed through widespread industry practice—or they can be standards formally promulgated by an industry body that represents many industry participants.[76]

To be clear, conformity with industry custom or practice is never dispositive; as one judge famously put it in a canonical negligence case, "A whole calling many have unduly lagged in the adoption of new and available [safety] devices."[77] Customary practice is nevertheless treated as strongly

---

[69] *See generally* Gary T. Schwartz, *The Myth of the Ford Pinto Case*, 43 Rutgers L. Rev. 1013 (1991) (discusses the Ford Pinto case, where Ford was found liable for a jury for placing the Ford Pinto on the market when presented with evidence that Ford sold the car with awareness of potential safety risks in the car).

[70] An example of a risk-utility test is the "Hand Test," famously articulated by Judge Learned Hand in *U.S. v. Carroll Towing*, 159 F.2d 169 (2d Cir. 1947). Under the Hand Test, a defendant breaches its duty of care by failing to take some precaution against inflicting a given injury if the burden of taking that precaution is outweighed by the probability of that accident occurring times the gravity of the injury. Conversely, a defendant met their burden of care if the cost of taking adequate precautions was greater than the probability of that accident occurring times the cost of the injury. Note that this test applies to negligence but is illustrative of the sort of risk-utility reasoning common in products liability.

[71] *See, e.g.*, Richard A. Posner, *A Theory of Negligence*, 1 J. Legal Stud. 29 (1972). Many of these economic accounts take inspiration from the "Hand Test."

[72] Mark Geistfeld, *Products Liability* 123 (2d ed. 2021).

[73] Stephen G. Gilles, *The Invisible Hand Formula*, 80 Va. L. Rev. 1015, 1018–19 (1994) ("Juries are told neither that a reasonable person is one who complies with community values and norms nor that a reasonable person is one who balances costs and benefits [or behaves "as if" balancing them]. Instead, the reasonable person standard is given to the jury without elaboration.").

[74] *Restatement (Third) of Torts: Phys. & Emot. Harm* § 13 (2010).

[75] Kenneth S. Abraham, *Custom, Noncustomary Practice, and Negligence*, 109 Colum. L. Rev. 1784, 1815 (2009) ("[B]y making reference to custom evidence, the typical jury instruction on custom emphasizes to the jury the potential probative value of this evidence.").

[76] *Restatement (Third) of Torts: Phys. & Emot. Harm* § 13 cmt. e (2010).

[77] *The T. J. Hooper*, 60 F.2d 737, 740 (2d Circ. 1932).

probative of what due care requires. Where industry custom is not settled—which may be the case, today, with respect to important aspects of AI development—juries may still take the actions of other industry participants into account when assessing the reasonableness of the defendant's behavior. If some industry actors routinely take precautions that would have reduced the chance of injury to the plaintiff, this may provide evidence that the defendant's failure to take similar precautions was unreasonable. Indeed, as one tort scholar famously observed, tort law treats industry custom as probative largely because it "sharpens attention on the practicality of caution greater than the defendant used."[78]

These facts have considerable significance for AI developers. In particular,

- **AI developers that fail to employ industry-leading safety practices, such as rigorous independent safety testing or the installation of robust safeguards against misuse,[79] may incur substantial liability exposure.** In the aftermath of harm caused by an AI system, juries, which skew toward safety considerations in their evaluations of reasonableness, may find AI developers liable for failing to utilize safety practices that would have foreseeably mitigated the risk of harm.[80] The more widespread these practices are, the more plausibly they constitute industry "custom," and the greater the risk of liability.[81] The line between industry practices that are "customary" and those that are not is unavoidably fuzzy. Moreover, as discussed above, industry safety practice helps to illuminate the requirements of reasonable care even when it is not sufficiently widespread to constitute custom: "The fact that an industry often takes a particular precaution is excellent evidence that the precaution is feasible and not excessively costly."[82] Thus, it may be hazardous for an AI developer to eschew *any* safety practice that has substantial currency within the industry (unless it employs some different safety practice that is demonstrably comparable in efficacy).[83]

- **More generally, AI developers are well advised to employ rigorous safety measures when deciding whether and how to train, store, or release a powerful new model.** Suppose, for instance, that in the future an AI developer decides to release the weights of an extremely powerful new model without carefully testing the model for risks of highly dangerous misuse,

---

[78] Clarence Morris, *Custom and Negligence*, 42 Colum. L. Rev. 1147, 1148 (1942).

[79] The United Kingdom has identified these techniques, among others, as best practices for managing the risks from advanced AI models and that leading AI companies have already committed to utilizing these practices. *See* U.K. Dept. for Sci., Innovation, and Tech., *Emerging Processes for Frontier AI Safety*, 4, 37 (Policy Paper, Oct. 27, 2023).

[80] Certain safety practices already exist to mitigate such risks. OpenAI, Google, and Anthropic all fine-tune their models to avoid harmful outputs. *See supra* note 15. Anthropic has participated in third-party safety evaluations and considers them an essential safety practice. Anthropic, *Third-Party Testing as a Key Ingredient of AI Policy* (March 25, 2024). Meta has published a series of benchmarks to "broadly measure and enhance the cybersecurity safety properties of LLMs." Manish Bhatt et al., *Purple Llama CyberSecEval: A Secure Coding Benchmark for Language Models*, arXiv 1 (2023). Google has proposed a battery of "dangerous capability" evaluations that can inform a developer when model release would be too dangerous. Mary Phuong et al., *Evaluating Frontier Models for Dangerous Capabilities*, arXiv (2024). For more on dangerous capabilities evaluations, see Shevlane et al., *supra* note 2.

[81] *Restatement (Third) of Torts: Phys. & Emot. Harm* § 13 cmt. e (2010).

[82] Dan B. Dobbs et al., *The Law of Torts* § 179 (2d ed. 2011).

[83] *Restatement (Third) of Torts: Phys. & Emot. Harm* § 13 cmt. c (2010).

or without equipping the model with reasonably effective safeguards against such misuse.[84] Suppose that such a bad actor subsequently downloads the model, removes its safeguards, and misuses it in a highly injurious fashion—for example, to conduct a cyberattack on critical infrastructure that results in many deaths or a great deal of property damage. The developer may be found to have breached its duty of care—especially if other developers *do* employ more rigorous precautions to guard against the use of their models to inflict such injuries.[85] Similar points apply, in a somewhat different form, to developers that do not release the weights of their models but instead provide access to them via APIs and web user interfaces.[86] If, for example, a malicious actor finds a way to circumvent the safeguards built into the model (or the interface through which it is accessed), the developer may face substantial liability risk—especially if other developers employ more rigorous forms of precaution to prevent their models from being improperly accessed and misused. That said, existing law on tort liability for third-party misuse is in important respects unclear and unsettled and differs across jurisdictions. Some of its complexities are discussed below.

- **Safety-focused policymakers, developers, and advocates can strengthen AI developers' incentives to employ cutting-edge safety techniques by developing, implementing, and publicizing new safety procedures and by formally promulgating these standards and procedures through industry bodies.** The popularization and proliferation of safe and secure AI development practices by safety-conscious developers and industry bodies can help to establish industry standards and "customs" that courts are likely to consider when evaluating the liability of other developers, creating stronger incentives for safe and responsible AI development.

---

[84] See Seger et al., *supra* note 11, for a discussion of the risks and benefits of open-sourcing powerful foundation models. On the removal of a model's safeguards through fine-tuning by malicious actors, see Gade et al., *supra* note 16; Simon Lerment et al., *LoRA Fine-Tuning Efficiently Undoes Safety Training in Llama 2-Chat 70B*, arXiv (2023). On the risk that safeguards might be inadvertently removed through fine-tuning by innocent actors, see Xiangyu Qi et al., *Fine-Tuning Aligned Language Models Compromises Safety, Even When Users Do Not Intend To!*, arXiv (2023).

[85] Leading AI developers have publicly agreed to rigorously test their models for safety risks, including risks of misuse, before their release. Courts might regard such agreements as helping to establish industry standards that inform the negligence determination. *See* U.K. Dept. for Sci., Innovation, and Tech., *supra* note 79, at 4 (noting that "many leading companies" agreed to conduct model evaluations and red-teaming of their products); *id.* at 17 (noting that models should be subject to "extensive pre-deployment evaluations"); *see also* Press Release, The White House, Biden-Harris Administration Secures Voluntary Commitments from Leading Artificial Intelligence Companies to Manage the Risks Posed by AI (July 21, 2023) (announcing that Amazon, Anthropic, Google, Inflection, Meta, Microsoft, and OpenAI had voluntarily committed to "internal and external security testing of their AI systems before their release").

[86] An API allows two computer programs to communicate with each other more easily and often provides a set of predefined mechanisms and tools to transmit data between programs. APIs are commonly used by businesses to allow third parties, such as other developers or customers, to interact directly with software stored on servers without selling copies directly to other parties. *See* Michael Goodwin, *What Is an API?*, IBM, https://www.ibm.com/topics/api (last visited Nov. 7, 2023). Several leading AI developers, such as OpenAI and Anthropic, use APIs in order to allow third parties, such as other firms and consumers, to interact with their models without allowing those third parties to gain possession of the models themselves (or derivative copies). A firm that provides access to a model through an API can monitor others to ensure that third parties are not using or modifying the model in dangerous ways. By contrast, if a firm decides to transfer a model to the possession of a third party, or open-source the model—i.e., post it on the open web such that third parties can freely download (a copy of) it—the firm will be unable to monitor how third parties subsequently use or modify it.

A comprehensive examination of developer liability for negligence would need to explore various issues that cannot be treated in depth here. The discussion below highlights some of these issues without fully exploring their subtleties or complexities.

Intervening Agency and Liability for Third-Party Misuse

In general, a defendant's action can "lack reasonable care" if the defendant's behavior "can foreseeably combine with or bring about the improper conduct of . . . a third party."[87] Nevertheless, courts sometimes hold that intervening wrongdoers "break the chain" of causation, thereby relieving negligent defendants of responsibility for the consequences of their actions.[88] In one famous case, the defendant's negligence caused an oil spill, and a third party threw a lighted cigar into the oil, causing a large explosion that injured the plaintiff.[89] Whether the defendant was liable to compensate the plaintiff, the court held, should be determined by whether the intervening agent acted negligently or maliciously. If the intervening agent had acted maliciously, the court held, then the defendant's action could not be regarded as the proximate cause of the plaintiff's injury, because the possibility of such a malicious action was "one which the appellees could not reasonably have anticipated or guarded against."[90]

An AI developer might make a parallel defensive argument if its model is maliciously used by a third party to, say, engage in cybercrime. But modern courts generally reject any "all-inclusive general rule" that malicious, tortious, or criminal intervening wrongdoing precludes negligence liability.[91] Instead, most courts maintain, liability generally turns on the foreseeability of the intervening agent's wrongful action, and on whether the defendant was duty-bound to guard against or refrain from enabling it.[92] As one leading commentary puts it, "If a criminal or intentional intervening act is foreseeable, or is part of the original risk negligently created by the defendant in the first place, then the harm is not outside the scope of the defendant's liability."[93] Similarly, the *Restatement (Third)* clarifies that "[i]f the third party's misconduct is among the risks making the defendant's conduct negligent, then ordinarily plaintiff's harm will be within the defendant's scope of liability."[94] So, for

---

[87] *Restatement (Second) of Torts* §§ 302A–B (1965).

[88] As a doctrinal matter, some courts treat intervening agency as a matter of proximate cause, and some treat it as a matter of duty. The distinction's main significance, in this context, is that it determines whether the issue will be decided by a judge or submitted to the jury.

[89] *Watson v. Kentucky & Indiana Bridge & R. Co.*, 137 Ky. 619, 624, *modified sub nom. Watson v. Kentucky & I. Bridge & R. Co.*, 137 Ky. 619 (1910), and abrogated by *Britton v. Wooten*, 817 S.W.2d 443 (Ky. 1991).

[90] *Id.* at 624.

[91] *Britton v. Wooten*, at 449.

[92] *Restatement (Third) of Torts: Phys. & Emot. Harm* § 19 (2010) ("The conduct of a defendant can lack reasonable care insofar as it foreseeably combines with or permits the improper conduct of the plaintiff or a third party.").

[93] Dobbs et al., *supra* note 82, § 209. *See also Craig v. Driscoll*, 262 Conn. 312, 813 A.2d 1003 (2003) ("[A] negligent defendant . . . is not relieved from liability by the intervention of another person, except where the harm is intentionally caused by the third person and is not within the scope of the risk created by the defendant's conduct. . . . Such tortious or criminal acts may in themselves be foreseeable . . . and so within the scope of the created risk.").

[94] *Restatement (Third) of Torts: Phys. & Emot. Harm* § 19 cmt. c (2010) ("If the third party's misconduct is among the risks making the defendant's conduct negligent, then ordinarily plaintiff's harm will be within the defendant's scope of liability. For

example, a federal district court in New York found that airline and security companies could be held liable for harms arising from the hijackings of airlines by terrorists on September 11, 2001, because these companies were obligated to take due care in screening passengers in order to guard against the risk of such events.[95] More recently, the Georgia Supreme Court found that a software company could be held liable for providing drivers with a software product that foreseeably induced reckless drivers to drive at unreasonable speeds.[96] In doing so, the Court explicitly disapproved a lower court's holding that "a manufacturer's duty to use reasonable care to design reasonably safe products 'does not extend to the intentional (not accidental) misuse of the product in a tortious way by a third party.'"[97] Instead, the Court clarified, "a manufacturer's design duty for purposes of a negligent-design claim extends to all reasonably foreseeable risks posed by a product."[98]

In the case of AI and potential harms it may cause, prominent voices in academia, government, and the AI industry are warning that powerful AI models may be maliciously misused in order to cause harm to personal safety and critical infrastructure and to engage in various other forms of criminal and tortious wrongdoing.[99] So, if a model is maliciously misused in one of these ways, it will be difficult for the defendant to argue that this eventuality was unforeseeable. Moreover, the fact that the large majority of leading AI developers install safeguards against such misuse will support both the claim that such misuse is foreseeable and the claim that AI developers are obligated to guard against it.

Doctrines about intervening agency will provide little help, moreover, if the intervening agent who misuses a developer's model is innocent or merely negligent. Suppose, for example, that a human instructs a model to achieve an inherently innocuous goal (such as making money online), and the model malfunctions by stealing digital assets in order to achieve this goal. Because the intervening human agent was at most negligent, the developer will be unable to claim that this human's action "broke the chain" of causation, or otherwise immunizes the developer from liability, even under more defendant-friendly understandings of intervening agency doctrine.[100] Perhaps the developer could claim that the *model* was a malicious intervening agent, for whose actions the developer should not be held liable. But it is highly uncertain, of course, whether courts will classify advanced AI systems as "agents" in this context; any such decision would mark a seismic development in the law. Moreover, this argument will be undermined by the fact that enabling models to engage in such misbehavior is a highly foreseeable consequence of developing or releasing them with inadequate safety protections.

---

example, if it is negligent to leave keys in one's unlocked car for a period of time in a high-crime area, at least in part because the car may foreseeably be stolen by someone who is likely to operate it negligently or recklessly, then the fact that the car is in fact stolen and driven negligently in a way that injures the plaintiff does not prevent a finding that plaintiff's harm is within the scope of defendant's liability for that negligence.").

[95] *In re Sept. 11 Litig.*, 280 F. Supp. 2d 279, 296–97 (S.D.N.Y. 2003) (that the hijacking of planes by the 9/11 hijackers was sufficiently foreseeable, and, therefore, "the injuries suffered by the ground victims arose from risks that were within the scope of the duty undertaken by the Aviation Defendants.").

[96] *Maynard v. Snapchat, Inc.*, 870 S.E.2d 739 (Ga. 2022).

[97] *Id.* at 748 (citing *Maynard v. Snapchat*, 357 Ga. App., at 500).

[98] *Id.* at 542.

[99] *See* Bengio et al., *supra* note 1; Center for AI Safety, *Statement on AI Risk*, https://www.safe.ai/statement-on-ai-risk (last visited Nov. 7, 2023).

[100] Dobbs et al., *supra* note 82, § 211.

Thus, a developer that fails to take reasonable precautions against third-party misuse of its models faces significant liability risk. However, when applying these principles to harms caused by AI, the magnitude of the risk that developers face is less than clear, for several reasons.

First, as previously mentioned, certain states (such as New York) hold that manufacturers of dangerous products cannot be held liable for third-party misuse of them if those products are misused only after substantial alteration.[101] If AI systems are treated as "products" for the purpose of products liability doctrine, or the relevant doctrine is treated as instructive, then developers whose models are stripped of installed safeguards may escape liability for resulting third-party misuse in these states. However, they will still face liability exposure in other states, such as California, which maintain that liability can attach if a third party's alteration and misuse of a product was reasonably foreseeable to the product manufacturer.[102]

Second, judges in many states have declined to allow suits against the manufacturers of certain other dangerous instrumentalities, such as guns, for negligently enabling third-party misuse of their products (e.g., in mass shootings).[103] Some judges reached this result by claiming that this third-party misuse of guns was not foreseeable, or sufficiently foreseeable, to incur liability.[104] Other judges forthrightly acknowledged that such misuse might be foreseeable, but nevertheless insulated gun manufacturers against liability for failing to take care against it. These judges were moved by concerns such as their view that gun manufacturers cannot realistically take effective precautions against such third-party misuse; that plaintiffs would not be able to establish the necessary causal connection between gun manufacturers' negligence and resulting harms from criminal misuse of their weapons; or that it would be socially undesirable to subject gun manufacturers to overly broad, "indeterminate" liability exposure.[105]

AI developers might hope that judges will shield them from negligence liability (i.e., prevent cases against them from reaching juries) on similar grounds. It would be unwise, however, for developers to assume they will be able to obtain any such judicial shield, for several reasons. First, it is plausible that AI developers *can* take reasonably effective precautions against enabling third-party misuse, even if available precautions are decidedly imperfect.[106] Second, several state courts *did* allow major cases

---

[101] *See Robinson v. Reed-Prentice Div. of Package Mach. Co.*, 403 N.E.2d 440 (N.Y. 1980) ("We hold that a manufacturer of a product may not be cast in damages, either on a strict products liability or negligence cause of action, where, after the product leaves the possession and control of the manufacturer, there is a subsequent modification which substantially alters the product and is the proximate cause of plaintiff's injuries.").

[102] *See* CACI No. 1245. Affirmative Defense—Product Misuse or Modification; *and supra* note 38.

[103] *See, e.g., Bloxham v. Glock Inc.*, 53 P.3d 196, 200 (Ct. App. Ariz. 2002) (finding that there was no duty for Glock to "control all sales at gun shows by third parties to third parties" and therefore Glock was not liable for negligent distribution of guns at such shows); *Hamilton v. Beretta U.S.A. Corp.*, 750 N.E.2d 1055, 1066, opinion after certified question answered, 264 F.3d 21 (2d Cir. 2001) (finding that handgun manufacturers owed no duty of reasonable care in marketing and distributing their guns to persons harmed with illegally obtained handguns); *City of Chicago v. Beretta U.S.A. Corp.*, 821 N.E.2d 1099, 1148 (Ill. 2004) (holding that gun manufacturers were not liable for public nuisance claims brought by Chicago for misuse of guns in the city by criminals); *Young v. Bryco Arms*, 821 N.E.2d 1078, 1091 (Ill. 2004) (holding that gun manufacturers were not liable under a theory of public nuisance for misuse of their products).

[104] *See, e.g., City of Chicago*, 821, at 1138 (finding that the alleged public nuisance caused by the distribution of guns was not "so foreseeable" that it could be deemed the legal cause of the alleged nuisance from criminal usage of the distributed guns).

[105] *See, e.g., Hamilton*, 750, at 1060; *Delahanty v. Hinckley*, 564 A.2d 758, 762 (D.C. 1989).

[106] *See supra* note 85 for some common precautions.

against gun manufacturers for the criminal misuse of their products to proceed to trial,[107] before Congress cut off ("preempted") such litigation by passing a wide-ranging federal statutory bar.[108] Third, courts that expressed hostility to gun manufacturer liability for third-party misuse were often influenced by factors such as the heavily regulated character of the gun industry.[109] The process of developing and releasing AI models, by contrast, is hardly regulated at all. Finally, some state legislatures (such as the California state legislature) have clarified, by statute, that gun manufacturers may indeed be sued for negligent practices that enable third-party misuse.[110] While these state statutory enactments cannot have their intended effect on gun manufacturer liability, because they are preempted by the aforementioned federal statute, these statutes (and the public policy determination they embody) might nevertheless be treated as probative by courts called to rule upon manufacturer liability for third-party misuse of other dangerous instrumentalities.

Judges may be especially likely to shield a model's developer from negligence liability in cases that involve a wrongdoer's use of a model to obtain *advice* (e.g., advice on software coding) that the wrongdoer subsequently uses to commit a wrong (e.g., creating and deploying a code cyberweapon to hack into a bank account). Holding a developer liable, in such circumstances, might engage First Amendment concerns about the protection of communication. As we discuss below, the First Amendment's application to AI models is a highly murky issue, which implicates basic but still unsettled questions in First Amendment doctrine as well as novel conceptual issues about the conditions under which AI output counts as "speech." First Amendment concerns might also lead judges to balk at subjecting developers to liability when their models are used to facilitate speech (or speech-like model activity), even wrongful speech.

In short, there is significant uncertainty about the scope and magnitude of developer liability for negligently enabling third parties to cause harm through model misuse. State legislatures might thus wish to enact legislation that clarifies (or modifies) the conditions under which developers will be held liable for the misuse of their models, or which clarifies the forms of precaution that due care against such misuse requires. Carefully crafted, well-targeted interventions in this area might strengthen legal incentives for responsible AI development while providing greater legal certainty to responsible developers, insurers, and other relevant parties.

That said, it may be difficult to identify—in advance of the litigation of concrete cases—normatively sound principles for determining when developers should and should not face liability for failing to guard against the misuse of their products. Existing legal standards about liability for misuse may be somewhat murky and unclear in application, but they are also flexible and dynamic—qualities that a more precise set of legal standards, enacted through legislation, would by their nature lack. Thus, we believe that legislatures would be well advised to proceed with considerable caution in this

---

[107] *See, e.g., City of Cincinnati v. Beretta U.S.A. Corp.*, 768 N.E.2d 1136, 1143–44 (Ohio 2002); *City of Gary ex rel. King v. Smith & Wesson Corp.*, 801 N.E.2d 1222, 1248 (Ind. 2003).

[108] Protection of Lawful Commerce in Arms Act, Pub. L. No. 109-92, 119 Stat. 2095 (2005) (codified at 15 U.S.C. §§ 7901-03 (2018)).

[109] *See, e.g., Bloxham v. Glock Inc.*, 53 P.3d 196, 200 (Ct. App. Ariz. 2002) ("Moreover, the firearms industry is highly regulated by the federal and state governments. . . . Imposing potential tort liability in a case such as this, which involves no regulatory violations, could ultimately conflict with firearms regulations.").

[110] *See* Giffords Law Center, *Gun Industry Immunity*, https://giffords.org/lawcenter/gun-laws/policy-areas/other-laws-policies/gun-industry-immunity/ (last visited Jan. 30, 2024).

area. While legislation could improve this difficult and murky area of law, it could also inhibit its ability to flexibly address situations that are difficult to analyze in advance.

Causation Issues

In order to recover, a tort plaintiff must show that her injury was caused by the defendant's negligent action.[111] Typically, this requires showing that the defendant's action was a "but-for" cause of the plaintiff's injury; the plaintiff must establish that they would not have suffered harm absent the defendant's action.[112] This may be difficult in some cases. To take an especially extreme and somewhat speculative example, suppose that a malicious actor uses an advanced AI system to facilitate the creation and deployment of a chemical weapon. It may be difficult for an injured plaintiff to establish which particular AI and developer was involved, particularly if the malicious actor concealed their activity or otherwise made it difficult to identify the AI system that he utilized. It may also be difficult for the plaintiff to establish that her injury traces to the use of an AI system at all, rather than knowledge that the malicious actor might have gained from a non-AI source.

The plaintiff will also need to demonstrate that their injury was caused by the defendant's *negligence*, as opposed to nonnegligent features of the defendant's action.[113] This might also present a hurdle to plaintiffs. Suppose, for example, that a model's safeguards are circumvented by a malicious actor who then misuses it, injuring the plaintiff. Even if the plaintiff can establish that the model's developer was negligent in failing to take additional precautions, it may be harder for the plaintiff to establish that the developer's failure to install such safeguards was the cause of the plaintiff's injury. In order to establish that legal fact, the plaintiff must show that, at least in principle, the model's safeguards would *not* have been circumvented (and the model subsequently misused so as to injure the plaintiff) if the defendant developer *had* installed adequately robust safeguards (or taken other suitable precautions).

For such reasons, proving causation may present an important obstacle to plaintiff recovery in some cases. At the same time, the magnitude of this obstacle should not be overstated. In practice, courts permit (and juries often make) fairly liberal inferences as to causation. As one leading commentary puts it, citing the *Restatement (Third)*, "Courts have often recognized, implicitly or explicitly, that the jury must be permitted to make causal judgments from its ordinary experience without demanding impossible proof about what would have occurred if the defendant had behaved more safely."[114] And of course, a plaintiff could establish that the defendant developer's negligence caused their injury if they can successfully argue that it was negligent to release such a dangerous model at all.

---

[111] *Restatement (Third) of Torts: Phys & Emot. Harm* § 26 (2010).

[112] *Id.* § 26 cmt. b (2010).

[113] *See Restatement (Second) of Torts* § 432(1) (1965); *see also* Dobbs et al., *supra* note 82, § 190 ("The specific act of negligence claimed by the plaintiff largely determines the hypothetical alternative conduct to be compared. If the plaintiff alleges that the defendant failed to keep a proper lookout, the hypothetical alternative case to be considered is one in which the defendant does keep a proper lookout and the question becomes whether, had he done so, he would have avoided injuring the plaintiff.").

[114] Dobbs et al., *supra* note 82, § 191 (citing *Restatement (Third) of Torts: Phys. & Emot. Harm* § 28 cmt. b (2010).

In other contexts, courts and legislatures have relaxed or modified traditional proof of causation requirements in order to facilitate the ability of injured plaintiffs to recover against demonstrably negligent plaintiffs. Legislatures might consider doing so in this context, as well. For example, a legislature could specify that, once a plaintiff has established that the defendant developer was negligent in developing, storing, or releasing a model, and that this model caused her injury, she does not *also* have the traditional burden of showing that the developer's *negligence* caused her injury.

The Dynamics of Jury Decisionmaking and Settlement

One final point, more practical than doctrinal, warrants mention. Different juries, empowered to decide potentially unclear questions of fact, may reach very different verdicts on the same set of facts, especially where those facts concern novel circumstances. These dynamics help to explain why most plausible negligence cases settle: The expected value of settling a somewhat plausible negligence claim rather than litigating it to judgment is often quite positive for a defendant—even if the claim is more likely to fail than succeed, and even if settlement will incur considerable financial cost. Thus, an action that is not in fact negligent, but which materially risks substantial physical harm or property damage to many people, might still incur substantial financial cost. For this reason, among others, even if AI developers were only subject to negligence liability (rather than any form of strict liability), they would be well advised to take great care to avoid causing harm to others at all.

This is especially true given that negligence determinations always occur after the fact; the reasonableness of a defendant's harmful behavior is always evaluated in hindsight. Even if it truly was reasonable for an AI developer to risk causing substantial harm to others, a jury may be inclined to find otherwise when faced with a plaintiff who has actually suffered such harm—especially if the developer has deep pockets, and the plaintiff is a sympathetic one. When the harm that has materialized is a catastrophic one—i.e., when the developer's actions have caused plaintiffs to suffer physical harm or property loss on a large scale—persuading the jury that unleashing this risk was a reasonable decision may be quite difficult.[115]

Conclusion

As we have discussed, the common-law tort of negligence is a source of significant liability risk for AI developers. It is uncertain how some significant areas of negligence doctrine—such as liability for third-party misuse of one's products—will apply to AI development. Nevertheless, there are concrete steps that developers can take to reduce their liability risk. In particular, since negligence doctrine accords great significance to industry custom and practice, developers can mitigate their liability exposure by employing industry-leading safety practices and standards. By the same token, AI developers, industry bodies, and policymakers who are concerned about safety can help to develop and promote compliance with safety-enhancing industry customs and standards, in order to strengthen industry incentives to take due care in developing and releasing powerful models.

---

[115] *See* Schwartz, *supra* note 69, at 103–45 (discussing the public's "ambivalent" attitude toward cost-benefit analysis, and the outrage felt toward Ford for placing a car model on the market knowing it would pose potential safety risks to passengers).

Chapter 4

Products Liability

While negligence is the most common form of tort case, the law also specializes in tort doctrines that come into play when courts adjudicate cases about the manufacture, design, or warnings provided in connection with items legally classified as "products" (rather than services, or items that are not "products," which are subject to the ordinary negligence standard). If courts or legislatures deem (certain) AI systems "products," these specialized doctrines would apply to AI development.

We begin by discussing some specialized products liability doctrines—the "risk-utility" version of design defect liability, and defective warning liability—that are close analogues to, or perhaps specialized versions of, negligence liability. Confusingly, these doctrines are sometimes called forms of "strict products liability," but most scholars and courts appear to agree that they are much closer in substance to negligence liability than genuinely strict liability.[116] Next, we discuss a specialized products liability doctrine—the "consumer expectations" version of design defect liability—i.e., by almost all accounts, genuinely strict in nature.

In certain cases, applying even negligence-like products liability doctrines (i.e., the risk-utility version of design defect liability and defective warning liability) may lead courts to reach different decisions about AI developer liability than they would have reached under the ordinary (nonproduct) negligence standard. Many states hold that ordinary negligence liability applies to product developers, alongside any specialized form of products liability to which they are also subject.[117] But in practice, courts deciding product cases often apply negligence-like "strict" products liability doctrines *instead of* ordinary negligence doctrines.[118] Thus, it makes sense to discuss these doctrines separately here.

---

[116] *See, e.g.*, Aaron Twerski & J. A. Henderson, *Achieving Consensus on Defective Product Design*, 83 Cornell L. Rev. 867, 871 (1998) (arguing that it is a "rhetorical confusion" to call the risk-utility version of design defect liability "strict" because most American courts effectively apply a negligence standard in making risk-utility products liability determinations). There is, to be fair, an important minority view that rejects this consensus. *See* Mark Geistfeld, *Strict Products Liability 2.0: The Triumph of Judicial Reasoning over Mainstream Tort Theory*, 14 J. Tort L. 403 (2021) (arguing that, notwithstanding scholarly consensus and judicial rhetoric to the contrary, design defect liability under the risk-utility test is—as a matter of actual judicial practice— genuinely a form of strict liability, which incorporates a cost-benefit balancing test that is somewhat similar to but importantly different from the cost-benefit test associated with the ordinary negligence standard).

[117] *See, e.g.*, *Blue v. Environmental Eng'g Inc.*, 828 N.E.2d 1128 (Ill. 2005); *Restatement (Second) of Torts* § 402A cmt. a (1965) ("The rule stated here is not exclusive and does not preclude liability based upon the alternative ground of negligence of the seller, where such negligence can be proved.").

[118] *See, e.g.*, *Golonka v. General Motors Corp.*, 65 P.3d 956, 965 (Ariz. Ct. App. 2003) ("When a plaintiff's claim for strict liability design and negligent design are factually identical, and the jury employs a risk/benefit analysis to determine that the manufacturer is not at fault of strict liability design, the jury cannot consistently find the product manufacturer at fault for negligent design.").

Are AI Systems "Products"?

A threshold question is whether (some) pieces of software, including AI models or systems, are "products" for the purposes of products liability law. The answer to this question is remarkably unclear and unsettled, and the answer may end up varying from state to state. Most judicial decisions on point appear to suggest that the answer is no.[119] But the majority of scholarly commentators, and perhaps some state courts, appear to hold that the answer is—or should be—yes. Many scholarly commentators argue that the functional rationales for subjecting the design of physical products to the specialized doctrines of products liability law support subjecting the design of software to products liability law as well. Moreover, it is especially plausible to maintain that software items that are incorporated into a physical product (such as an autonomous vehicle) *do* count as "products" subject to products liability.[120] That is because the components of "products" are themselves generally treated as "products," and thus subject to assessment as defective or nondefective under specialized products liability doctrine.[121] Finally, even if a court maintains that AI systems (or software items more generally) are *not* products subject to products liability law, it may nevertheless find products liability doctrine instructive and persuasive when elaborating on how largely similar negligence doctrines should apply to AI systems. For all of these reasons, it is worth considering how specialized products liability doctrines might apply to AI.

There are three forms of products liability: *manufacturing defect* liability, *design defect* liability, and liability for *failure to warn*. Manufacturing defect liability is less likely to be relevant to AI systems, so we set it aside here.[122] We will accordingly focus on doctrines concerning design defect liability and failure to warn liability.

---

[119] *See*, most recently, *Rodgers v. Christie*, 795 Fed. App'x 878, 879 (3d Cir. Mar. 6, 2020) (affirming district court's holding that a software program is not a product under the New Jersey Products Liability Act). *See also Intellect Art Multimedia, Inc. v. Milewski*, 899 N.Y.S.2d 60, 2009 WL 2915273, *7 (Sup. Ct. 2009) ("[P]laintiff has failed to demonstrate that, as a matter of law, the Ripoff Report website is a product so that Xcentric should be held strictly liable for any "injury" caused thereby."). *Restatement (Third) of Torts: Prod. Liab.* § 19 (1998) notes that products are "tangible personal property," while software is generally not considered tangible. *Restatement (Third) of Torts: Prod. Liab.* § 19 cmt. d (1998) notes that courts have not found software to be a product for the purposes of products liability rules.

[120] *See, e.g.,* Rebecca Crootof, *The Internet of Torts: Expanding Civil Liability Standards to Address Corporate Remote Interference,* 69 Duke L.J. 583, 667 n.209 (2019) (explaining that "[w]hile software has traditionally not been considered a product, an IoT device's integration of software with a physical object raises the issue of whether it is a component part subject to strict liability for defects.").

[121] *Restatement (Third) of Torts: Prod. Liab.* § 5 (1998); *see also Zaza v. Marquess & Nell, Inc.,* 675 A.2d 620, 629 (N.J. 1996) (discussing the majority rule that component part manufacturers are generally immune from liability when their non-defective parts are integrated into a larger product).

[122] Manufacturing defect liability applies when a product causes injury by failing to function in accordance with its intended design. Such liability is strict, rather than based on negligence or fault: Even if a bottle manufacturer takes all due care to carefully design, manufacture, and distribute its bottles, it may still put at least a few "lemons" (i.e., defectively manufactured bottles) on the market, and it is liable for any injuries caused to consumers or bystanders by these lemons. We set manufacturing defect liability aside because it is unlikely to have much application to AI systems, which cause harm (whether directly or through misuse) because of how they have been designed—i.e., what algorithmic architectures they utilize, what processes were used to train their weights, what safeguards were installed in them through fine-tuning, and so on.

Design Defect Liability: The Risk-Utility Test

There are currently two tests for design defect: the *consumer expectations test* and the *risk-utility test*. A substantial minority of states, following the prescription of the *Restatement (Third)*, relies entirely on the risk-utility test.[123] A much smaller number of states relies entirely on the consumer expectations test.[124] The majority of states permit plaintiffs to invoke either test in order to establish design defect, or else utilize a hybrid of the two tests.[125]

The risk-utility test is typically characterized by courts and commentators as a close analogue to ordinary (nonproducts) negligence liability—so close, in fact, that some regard it as negligence liability under a different name.[126] By contrast, the consumer expectations test is generally regarded as a genuinely strict form of liability.

Given that the risk-utility test for design defect is very similar to the ordinary negligence standard, it is not surprising that much risk-utility doctrine seems directly relevant and instructive for determining whether AI developers are negligent. In particular, there is a rich body of risk-utility jurisprudence that addresses whether and when the manufacturer of a dangerous instrumentality must install safety devices that protect against its misuse. As one leading commentary explains,

> a product may be defectively designed if it lacks devices which are necessary in order to make it reasonably safe, and a product may be defective in design if the manufacturer fails to incorporate feasible safety features to prevent foreseeable injuries. Thus, a design that presents unreasonable hazards within the range of the equipment's foreseeable uses imposes an additional duty on the designer-manufacturer to provide adequate guards against those hazards.[127]

What this duty requires is sensitive, however, to the costs (financial or otherwise) of installing the additional safeguards: "The trier of the fact must weigh the manufacturer's ability to minimize and/or eliminate the unsafe character of the product against the degree or amount of impairment in its usefulness any safeguards would cause."[128] Because installing safeguards against misuse in an AI system could also reduce its ability to serve innocuous ends,[129] courts might draw upon such precedents in determining whether an AI developer's failure to install more-robust safeguards against misuse constituted a violation of the risk-utility test.

There are, however, other features of design defect products liability analysis that distinguish it from ordinary (nonproduct) negligence analysis, and these doctrines may give rise to analytical confusion or difficulties in the context of advanced AI systems. Courts are readily prepared to find

---

[123] *Branham v. Ford Motor Co.*, 701 S.E.2d 5, 14 n.12, 15 (S.C. 2010) (the risk-utility test is the exclusive test of design defect liability in 17 states).

[124] *Id.* at 14–15 & n.11 ("By our count 35 of the 46 states that recognize strict products liability utilize some form of risk-utility analysis in their approach to determine whether a product is defectively designed.").

[125] *Id.* at 14–15.

[126] *See supra* note 116.

[127] *American Law of Products Liability* § 28:100 (Russell J. Davis et al., eds., 3d ed. 1987).

[128] *Id.* § 28:105.

[129] *See, e.g.*, Alexander Wei et al., *Jailbroken: How Does LLM Safety Training Fail?*, arXiv 9 (2023) (noting a possible trade-off between capabilities and safety).

that a product manufacturer should have chosen an alternative product design, because the risk-utility profile of the design it *did* choose was less favorable than the proposed alternative. Thus, a court might find that an advanced AI system (e.g., a powerful model accessible through an API) is defectively designed because it contains inadequate safeguards against misuse, as more-diligent safety testing might have revealed. In general, however, courts are hesitant to find that an *entire category of products* is defective, even if the benefits of putting such a product on the market very plausibly outweigh the benefits of doing so.[130]

An AI developer, which open-sources its model by making key components of its model (such as the model weights) publicly available for download, might thus argue that an open-source model is simply a different category of product altogether from a closed-source system (such as a model accessed through an API whose weights are not available).[131] If this argument convinces a judge, he might rule that the developer is exempt from design defect liability, and dismiss the case before it reaches the jury—even if the jury would plausibly find that the developer's decision to open-source a powerful dual-use model was negligent because, say, its safeguards against extreme misuse are easily removable through fine-tuning. That is because it is arguable that open-source models, by their very nature, *cannot* be equipped with safeguards against misuse that are more resistant to removal: Currently, at least, to open-source a model is ipso facto to render it vulnerable to easy alteration by any third party with the modicum of technical sophistication necessary to engage in elementary forms of fine-tuning.[132] By contrast, if a court were to find that open-sourced models and models-accessed-via-API represent two different instances of a *single product category*, there would be no such barrier to a finding of design defect under the risk-utility test. Arguably, it does not make much sense for negligence liability to depend on this sort of quasi-metaphysical distinction between different categories of product on the one hand and different instances of a single product category on the other. But making such distinctions is part and parcel of existing design defect jurisprudence: Judgments about categorical liability involve "thorny questions of identity and definition" that are, for the most part, "practically impossible to settle in the abstract."[133] The analysis may look quite different if a court applies ordinary (non–products liability) negligence doctrine instead.

A more general upshot of this discussion is this: Because it is unsettled whether AI systems are "products"—and because there are some significant divergences between design defect products liability doctrine and ordinary (nonproduct) negligence liability doctrine—there is a significant amount of uncertainty about how some critical threshold issues about AI developer liability will be resolved. Moreover, because these issues may be resolved differently in different states, AI developers

---

[130] *Restatement (Third) of Torts: Prod. Liab.* § 2 cmt. d, rep.'s note (1998) ("The requirement that a plaintiff establish that the product that caused harm was defectively manufactured, was inadequately designed, or was not accompanied by adequate instructions or warnings, applies in most instances even when the plaintiff alleges that the product was egregiously dangerous. Comment e recognizes the possibility that egregiously dangerous products might be held defective for that reason alone. But a clear majority of courts that have faced the issue have refused to hold."). For goods such as firearms, it may be impossible to reduce much of the danger with a "reasonable alternative design" without also compromising the products' functionality, and hence courts have generally declined to find an entire category of products defective even if the goods are generally dangerous. While some courts have applied such categorical liability, they are a distinct minority.

[131] *See supra* note 13 and accompanying text for a discussion of model weights.

[132] *See* Seger et al., *supra* note 11.

[133] *In re DePuy Orthopaedics, Inc., Pinnacle Hip Implant Prod. Liab. Litig.*, 888 F.3d 753, 766–67 (5th Cir. 2018).

will likely be subject to considerable uncertainty and liability risk with respect to these issues for the foreseeable future.

Design Defect Liability: The Consumer Expectations Test and the Malfunction Doctrine

The consumer expectations test evaluates a product's design by reference to the ordinary consumer's safety expectations: The product's design is defective if it is dangerous to a degree, or in a way, not contemplated by the ordinary consumer (i.e., the ordinary purchaser or user).[134] If a product fails to perform as safely as an ordinary consumer would expect, it is defective under the consumer expectations test,[135] and both consumers and bystanders may recover for resulting injuries. The paradigmatic application of consumer expectations doctrine is to products that are, in an intuitively clear sense, *malfunctioning*.[136] Courts frequently struggle to clearly articulate exactly what it means for a product to "malfunction" and often limit themselves to providing intuitively clear examples: "The steering mechanism of a new automobile should not cause the car to swerve off the road; the drive shaft of a new automobile should not separate from the vehicle when it is driven in a normal manner; the brakes of a new automobile should not suddenly fail; and the accelerator of a new automobile should not stick without warning, causing the vehicle suddenly to accelerate."[137]

Certain catastrophic or large-scale harms would seem to fit this paradigm. It seems highly plausible that, if an AI model escapes its users' control and begins to propagate and self-replicate online because of accidental or deliberate programming of such behavior—causing damage to important digital infrastructure and digital property interests—the model is fairly characterized as malfunctioning and acting more dangerously than ordinary consumers expect. In other cases of large-scale AI harm, however, the consumer expectation test may provide less help to injured plaintiffs. For one thing, many commentators maintain that "the utility of the consumer expectations test is severely compromised when design dangers are obvious. Because consumers acquire their safety and danger expectations most directly from a product's appearance, obvious dangers—such as the risk to human limbs from an unguarded power mower or industrial machine—are virtually always contemplated or expected by the user or consumer."[138] If an advanced AI model has some plainly and obviously dangerous feature, therefore, plaintiffs injured by it may struggle to obtain recovery under the consumer expectations test. That said, they might still be able to recover under the risk-utility test (which many states apply alongside the consumer expectations test, as an alternative basis of design defect liability) or under the ordinary negligence standard.

The consumer expectation test's ability to provide plaintiffs with recovery may also be hostage to common societal understanding. If some dangerous propensity of a class of advanced AI systems becomes sufficiently common knowledge, it will become less plausible to maintain that harms resulting

---

[134] *Restatement (Second) of Torts* § 402A cmts. i & g (1965).

[135] *Soule v. General Motors Corp.*, 882 P.2d 298, 304 (Cal. 1994).

[136] Geistfeld, *supra* note 72, at 93–106.

[137] *Phipps v. General Motors Corp.*, 363 A.2d 955, 959 (Md. 1976) (citations omitted).

[138] David G. Owen & Mary J. Davis, *Owen & Davis on Products Liability* § 8:5 (4th ed. 2022).

from this dangerous propensity flout the actual expectations of the ordinary or average consumer. As the dangers of powerful AI systems become more evident and more widely understood, therefore, the consumer expectations test may supply progressively less propitious a basis for plaintiff recovery.

Finally, on certain understandings of design defect liability under the consumer expectation test, an AI developer may be able to avoid liability by providing appropriate warnings about an AI system's inherent risks. For it is arguable that, if a consumer has been adequately warned about such a risk, the consumer "cannot have frustrated expectations in the event that the risk materializes," for which reason liability under the consumer expectations test is foreclosed.[139] On this view, an AI developer that provides a sufficiently clear warning that an advanced AI system could conceivably begin to resist its users' control, and thereby cause them to suffer damage, might escape liability under the consumer expectations test should this risk materialize. Even if so, however, recovery might still be possible under the risk-utility test (which, to repeat, many states apply alongside the consumer expectations test, as an alternative basis of design defect liability) or the ordinary negligence standard.

Despite these possible limitations, the consumer expectations test is a source of liability exposure that AI developers should take seriously. Where the test applies, plaintiffs will be able to establish a claim for recovery without encumbrance by various burdensome doctrinal requirements associated with the ordinary negligence standard and the risk-utility standard. In particular, plaintiffs will not need to establish that the developer's decisions were negligent. Nor will they need to establish that their injuries were caused by the negligent aspect of the developer's decisions. Such plaintiffs will only need to establish that their injuries were caused by the feature of the model that violated their expectations of safe performance.

Another closely related potential source of recovery is worth mentioning. As previously stated, some courts follow the *Restatement (Third)* in rejecting the consumer expectations test entirely, in favor of the risk-utility test. Importantly, however, section 3 of the *Restatement (Third)* allows an injured plaintiff to recover, even if she cannot demonstrate that the product's expected utility was outweighed by its riskiness, "when the incident that harmed the plaintiff: (a) was of a kind that ordinarily occurs as a result of product defect; and (b) was not, in the particular case, solely the result of causes other than product defect existing at the time of sale or distribution."[140] The comments to this section clarify that it covers cases in which a product has manifestly malfunctioned in the sense of failing to perform its "manifestly intended function, thus supporting the conclusion that a defect of some kind is the most probable explanation."[141] The idea is that a plaintiff should be relieved of her burden to specifically establish that the defendant failed the risk-utility test when a malfunction provides strong circumstantial evidence for this proposition.[142] Various state courts have explicitly adopted this section of the *Restatement (Third)*,[143] and others might treat it as instructive in appropriate cases.

---

[139] Mark A. Geistfeld, *A Roadmap for Autonomous Vehicles: State Tort Liability, Automobile Insurance, and Federal Safety Regulation*, 105 Calif. L. Rev. 1611, 1639 (2017).

[140] *Restatement (Third) of Torts: Prod. Liab.* § 3 ("Circumstantial Evidence Supporting Inference of Product Defect") (1998).

[141] *Id.* cmt. b.

[142] *Id.* § 3.

[143] *See, e.g., Pitts v. Genie Indus., Inc.*, 921 N.W.2d 597, 598 (Neb. 2019).

Some cases in which an AI system directly causes harm by behaving in an unintended and undesirable manner might qualify. Suppose, for example, that a highly advanced AI system unexpectedly replicates itself,[144] without any instruction to do so by its user; infects many web servers; and thereby causes damage to a plaintiff's digital property. The plaintiff might plausibly argue that the system has malfunctioned in the sense contemplated by section 3 of the *Restatement (Third)*, since the manufacturer did not intend for the system to replicate itself without instruction from the user. In response, however, the defendant might argue that this event is not "of a kind that *ordinarily occurs* as a result of product defect"—that is, because the event is unprecedented, it fails to provide strong circumstantial evidence that the risks of releasing the system outweighed its expected benefits. Both arguments seem colorable. Thus, the various states that have adopted section 3 of the *Restatement (Third)* might adjudicate this issue differently.

Liability for Defective Warnings

Defective warning products liability jurisprudence may also have implications for AI developers. This may be true even if courts do not classify AI systems as products, for they may nevertheless draw on products liability jurisprudence in order to elaborate on the scope and content of model developers' negligence liability for failing to provide reasonable warnings.

According to the *Restatement (Third)*, a product is "defective because of inadequate instructions or warnings when the foreseeable risks of harm posed by the product could have been reduced or avoided by the provision of reasonable instructions or warnings by the seller or other distributor, or a predecessor in the commercial chain of distribution, and the omission of the instructions or warnings renders the product not reasonably safe."[145] If a product is used in a way that the provision of an appropriate warning would have disincentivized or otherwise prevented, the seller or distributor may be liable to compensate those (whether the product's users or bystanders) who suffer injury as a result. Suppose, then, that an AI developer open-sources its model by posting the model's weights online, without warning that fine-tuning the weights may inadvertently remove some of their built-in safeguards against exhibiting undesirable behavior.[146] Suppose, moreover, that these safeguards prevent the model in question from engaging in undesirable and unintended forms of manipulation or deception. If an innocent actor downloads the model's weights, fine-tunes it in a way that inadvertently removes these safeguards, and the model subsequently engages in manipulation or deception of the innocent actor or third parties, the model developer may be liable for resulting harm. That is because it might plausibly be argued, in such a scenario, that the open-source developer was obligated to warn

---

[144] For an evaluation of current AI agents' abilities to self-replicate, see, e.g., Megan Kinniment et al., *Evaluating Language-Model Agents on Realistic Autonomous Tasks*, arXiv (2023).

[145] *Restatement (Third) of Torts: Prod. Liab.* § 2 (1998). An obligation to warn other parties of certain risks has also been recognized in negligence law in other contexts, such as requiring warnings for certain risks on land someone owns. *See Restatement (Second) of Torts* § 342 (1965) (a possessor of land must warn licensees, those they give permission to enter their land, of risks on that land).

[146] Qi et al., *supra* note 84, at 1 ("[E]ven without malicious intent, simply fine-tuning with benign and commonly used datasets can also inadvertently degrade the safety alignment of LLMs, though to a lesser extent . . . even if a model's initial safety alignment is impeccable, it is not necessarily to be maintained after custom fine-tuning."). On fine-tuning, see *supra* note 13 and accompanying text.

that fine-tuning the weights might render the model unsafe or render it unsafe in this particular way. There is, however, a colorable argument that such a warning would itself pose unreasonable risks of harm, by alerting bad actors to the possibility of fine-tuning out a model's safeguards.[147] If courts find such arguments convincing, they may hold that providing such warnings is *not* required.

Courts have not yet opined, of course, on the nature and level of detail of the warnings that must be provided in the context of advanced AI development. How these matters will ultimately be resolved is highly uncertain. In general, it is difficult to predict, in advance, what sorts of warnings will be deemed necessary: "In evaluating the adequacy of product warnings and instructions, courts must be sensitive to many factors. It is impossible to identify anything approaching a perfect level of detail that should be communicated in product disclosures."[148] The difficulty is exacerbated in this context by the novelty and rapid development of the technology at issue.

For plaintiffs, warning defect claims have an important strategic advantage: Warning defect liability operates with different and less demanding causal standards than other forms of liability. Suppose an injured plaintiff successfully argues that the defendant developer failed to provide an adequate warning, to the model's users, of some risk of unsafe behavior that the developer knew (or should have known) inhered in the model. If this risk should materialize and injure the plaintiff, once the model is used (by the plaintiff or anyone else), then the plaintiff will be able to recover for the injuries they have suffered *even if the user would have used it and unleashed the risk despite being warned of it.* In other words, the defendant's failure to adequately warn need not be shown to be counterfactually relevant to the consumer's decision to use the product, and the plaintiff's subsequent injury, in order for the plaintiff to recover.[149]

For these reasons, the fact that many developers appear to omit material warnings regarding the safety risks of using or fine-tuning their models may be a source of significant liability risk. As previously noted, this liability exposure would not disappear if courts should decline to classify AI models as products subject to specialized products liability doctrine, for defective warning jurisprudence will still supply a plausible template for courts that must decide what reasonable care requires in this domain.

Conclusion

Whether and how the specialized doctrines of products liability law will be applied to AI is highly uncertain. Much depends on which AI systems will be defined as products; while it is quite likely that those incorporated into physical products will be so defined, it is much less likely that those not incorporated into physical products will be so defined. Moreover, products liability doctrines differ substantially from jurisdiction to jurisdiction: some use the "risk-utility" test, some use the consumer expectations test, and many use some hybrid of both. Under the risk-utility test, the liability of AI developers will be determined in *largely* the same way as under traditional negligence doctrine—but

---

[147] We thank Mark Geistfeld for raising this point.

[148] *See Restatement (Third) of Torts: Prod. Liab.* § 2 (1998).

[149] *See Watkins v. Ford Motor Co.*, 190 F.3d 1213, 1219 (11th Cir. 1999) ("Although a warning may have the net effect of preventing an accident, that is not what is required by the law. The law merely requires the warning to inform the consumer of the nature and existence of the hazard, allowing him to make an informed decision whether to take on the risks warned of.").

with some important differences, as we have discussed. Under the consumer expectations test, it will plausibly be easier for injured plaintiffs to hold developers liable, since they will not need to establish that an AI system was faultily designed, developed, or released. Developers that wish to gauge and mitigate their tort liability risk will need to attend to these potential forms of liability and pay particular attention to ensuring that their models behave in line with users' expectations and providing adequate warnings of what behaviors their models could undertake.

Chapter 5

Strict Liability for Abnormally Dangerous Activities

In addition to the doctrines of negligence and products liability, tort law subjects certain abnormally or highly dangerous activities—such as the use of certain explosives, and the keeping of certain wild animals as pets—to a rule of strict liability. If an actor engages in such an activity and thereby (proximately) causes harm to another person's body or property, the actor will be liable to compensate the victim even if they took all due care to avoid harm. If the actor *has* demonstrably failed to take due care, he may be held liable in negligence, as well.

Courts and commentators characterize the class of activities that will incur such strict liability as *abnormally dangerous* or *ultrahazardous*. A central motivation for recognizing this form of strict liability is that some activities pose inherent and significant safety risks, even when the activities are undertaken with all due care and all reasonable precautions. In determining whether an activity is subject to abnormally dangerous activity (ADA) strict liability, courts consider several factors, including the level of risk posed by the actions, the magnitude of harm posed by the actions, the inability to eliminate risks by exercising reasonable care, how common the activity is, and the social value of the activity.[150]

It is plausible (although controversial) that developing and releasing very powerful AI systems (such as highly capable foundation models and certain, high-risk narrow AI models, such as biological design tools)[151] imposes risks of a different kind and greater magnitude than the risks entailed by ordinary commercial or scientific activity.[152] Moreover, it is possible to argue that the development and release of the most powerful AI models is not an activity in "common usage," given that the development of such powerful models is occurring within a very small number of labs.[153] It is possible, therefore, that at least some states' courts might characterize the activities of developing or releasing the most powerful models as an abnormally dangerous or ultrahazardous activities subject to ADA strict liability. There are several doctrinal and practical reasons, however, that courts might refrain from embracing this idea, or embrace it only in limited form.

---

[150] *Restatement (Second) of Torts* § 519 (1977).

[151] Bommasani et al., *supra* note 12; *see also supra* note 2.

[152] See *supra* note 1 for some potential risks of advanced AI development.

[153] While this argument is certainly colorable, it is far from obviously correct, and it may lose its power as such models become more numerous and more fully integrated into important societal infrastructure. *See Restatement (Third) of Torts: Phys. & Emot. Harm* § 20 cmt. j (2010) ("[A]ctivities can be in common use even if they are engaged in by only a limited number of actors. Consider the company that transmits electricity through wires, or distributes gas through mains, to most buildings in the community. The activity itself is engaged in by only one party. Even so, electric wires and gas mains are pervasive within the community. Moreover, most people, though not themselves engaging in the activity, are connected to the activity; electric wires and gas mains reach their homes. Accordingly, the activity is obviously in common usage, and partly for that reason strict liability is not applicable.").

First, courts have generally been very hesitant to expand the list of activities that are subject to ADA strict liability, even when confronted with activities that are plausibly just as dangerous as those activities (such as blasting) that *are* subject to ADA strict liability.[154]

Second, courts have rarely held that the *seller* or *distributor* of a dangerous entity or instrumentality, as opposed to its *owner* or *possessor*, is subject to ADA strict liability for resulting harms. (Sellers and distributors of commercial products may be subject to "strict products liability," which is, despite its name, often much less strict in character. Products liability is discussed in the previous chapter.) For example, although detonating certain explosives is subject to ADA strict liability, manufacturing or selling such explosives is not. In this respect, analogous precedent does not support holding that an AI developer that transfers a model, by open-sourcing it or transferring (a copy of) it to a purchaser, is subject to ADA strict liability for the harms that result from its use. Similarly, under existing doctrine, courts would be hesitant to subject a developer to liability for harms resulting from the illegal misuse of a model taken from its possession.[155] That said, such a theft might raise a strong inference that the developer took inadequate precautions in securing and storing the model, and thereby subject the developer to negligence liability.

This leaves open the possibility that a developer who maintains possession and control of a model (e.g., because the developer allows access to it only via an API, which the developer monitors and controls) could be subject to ADA strict liability. To subject only such developers to ADA strict liability, however, would seem to create a curious asymmetry between closed-source and open-source model developers—indeed, one that would incentivize a kind of model release (i.e., open-source) that is arguably more dangerous. It is difficult to predict how courts might react to this observation, but it might lead some courts to refrain from subjecting *any* form of model release (open-source or closed-source) to ADA strict liability.

Third, an important factor that courts consider in deciding whether to classify an activity as abnormally dangerous is its net social value—or, as the *Restatement (Second)* puts it, the "extent to which its value to the community is outweighed by its dangerous attributes."[156] The case for ADA liability is at its strongest when dealing with an activity, such as keeping wild beasts in a domestic environment, that is of dubious societal value. Conversely, the greater the societal value of an activity, the less likely courts will subject it to ADA liability. It is plausible that there is significant societal value in developing and releasing powerful AI models. Of course, it is plausible that this activity also creates significant societal dangers—dangers that might, in the case of sufficiently powerful and dangerous models, outweigh the societal value of releasing them (or releasing them except in extremely cautious ways). But courts might hesitate to subject the development and release of powerful models

---

[154] *Restatement (Second) of Torts: Phys. & Emot. Harm* § 20 cmt. e (1977) (explaining the classification of blasting as abnormally dangerous). The manufacture and sale of guns has never been considered an abnormally dangerous activity because courts emphasize that "it is not the sale of guns itself that is dangerous, but rather their improper use." *Restatement (Second) of Torts: Phys. & Emot. Harm* § 20 rep.'s note g (1977). Cases have emphasized that danger must be "inherent in the activity itself" rather than arising from improper use. *Burkett v. Freedom Arms, Inc.*, 704 P.2d 118, 121 (Or. 1985). The *Restatement* emphasizes that many plausibly abnormally dangerous activities, such as running railroad tracks for storage of chemicals, have not been classified as such by courts. *Restatement (Second) of Torts: Phys. & Emot. Harm* § 20 rep.'s note g (1977).

[155] *See, e.g., Bridges v. Parrish*, 742 S.E.2d 794, 798 (2013) ("The mere possession of a legal yet dangerous instrumentality does not create automatic liability when a third party takes that instrumentality and uses it in an illegal act.").

[156] *Restatement (Second) of Torts* § 519 (1977).

to ADA liability on this basis, given that the nature and magnitude of these dangers remain controversial and uncertain.

Despite these points, courts might be more willing to find that a developer is subject to ADA strict liability for harms caused by a powerful model that has *escaped* from the developer's possession and control in some fashion. In the wake of such an event, the analogy to a wild beast that escapes its owner's custody may be especially persuasive. Moreover, if a powerful model has caused sufficiently widespread and catastrophic harm, courts might be willing to impose ADA liability on its developer even if the model caused such harm only after it was sold or distributed.

In conclusion, there is little precedent for holding that the seller or distributor of a dangerous entity is subject to ADA strict liability for harms that it causes after distribution or sale. But there is no bright-line rule that *precludes* such a determination. And if such a model causes a catastrophic loss of life or property, the propositions that would support ADA liability in this context will likely seem much more compelling. That is, in the wake of such a catastrophe, the activity of developing and releasing such models might be widely regarded as unusually dangerous; difficult to make safe, even with all due care; and more dangerous than its value to the community warrants.

Chapter 6

Public Nuisance

Plaintiffs may also look to other, specialized tort doctrines beyond strict liability to respond to large-scale harms from AI if and when they become increasingly common. One particular tort, that of public nuisance, has been used to address large-scale harms from other causes, and might be utilized to respond to large-scale harms from AI. In recent decades, state attorneys general and plaintiffs' attorneys have started to utilize public nuisance to sue the manufacturers and distributors of dangerous substances or instrumentalities. A public nuisance consists in "an unreasonable interference with a right common to the general public."[157] While the tort was originally "developed in medieval England to allow the Crown to remove impediments from public roads and waterways,"[158] it has served in recent decades as the basis for ambitious attempts to hold the manufacturers and distributors of tobacco, opioids, guns, lead paint, subprime loans, greenhouse gasses, and chemical pollutants of waterways responsible for the harm their products have (putatively) caused to public health and welfare.[159] Unlike other tort causes of action, public nuisance actions can be brought by state officials, acting on behalf of the people they represent, along with private attorneys representing those who have suffered "special injuries" from the public nuisance alleged, with large settlements and damages sometimes resulting from such cases, such as in recent public nuisance cases over the distribution of opioids.[160]

If an AI model causes harm to many members of the public, it is possible that public nuisance claims will be brought alongside claims in negligence. That is because the tort of public nuisance offers litigants seeking tort recovery several substantive and procedural advantages over negligence and other torts.

First, while most of the defendants in prominent public nuisance cases have arguably behaved in a negligent manner (or worse), public nuisance is in theory a strict liability tort—the defendant need not be at fault in order to be liable in public nuisance for the harms it has caused.[161] Bringing a claim in public nuisance rather than negligence may thus relieve plaintiffs of the burden to establish that the defendant owed them a duty of care, that it was negligent, and that the negligent feature of its action caused them to suffer injury. Furthermore, a distinctive feature of public nuisance actions is that they can be brought by state officials, in addition to private parties. If a developer's AI model causes mass-

---

[157] *Restatement (Second) of Torts* § 821B (1979).

[158] Leslie Kendrick, *The Perils and Promise of Public Nuisance*, 132 Yale L.J. 702, 706 (2023) (citing *Restatement (Second) of Torts* § 821B cmt. a (1979)).

[159] *Id.* at 706.

[160] For a comprehensive list of settlements paid in opioid litigation to state plaintiffs, see Christine Minhee, *States' Opioid Settlement Statuses*, Opioid Settlement Tracker, https://www.opioidsettlementtracker.com/globalsettlementtracker (last visited Jan. 30, 2024).

[161] Kendrick, *supra* note 158, at 758.

scale harm, therefore, state officials might bring claims in public nuisance against that developer, alongside whatever claims are brought against the developer by private litigants. Since it is often the case that "state officials can muster more effective legal resources than individual litigants,"[162] such public nuisance claims by state officials might be more effective in securing large verdicts or settlements.

Third, for technical doctrinal reasons that need not detain us here, plaintiffs have sometimes been able to recover for pure economic loss (i.e., financial loss unconnected to any underlying bodily harm or property damage) by bringing their claims in public nuisance.[163] By contrast, as already discussed, liability in negligence does not extend to pure economic loss except in unusual cases. Since a defendant's negligent action will often cause vastly more pure economic loss than personal injury or property damage (or economic loss that derives from them), an AI developer successfully sued in public nuisance can expect to face a much larger financial burden than a developer successfully sued only in negligence (or under other tort causes of action, such as ADA strict liability).

The specter of public nuisance suits should thus be of concern to AI developers whose models might cause large-scale harm to the public. As noted above, while many public nuisance suits against manufacturers and distributors of dangerous instrumentalities have been rejected by judges, a good portion have been allowed to go to trial and resulted in large settlements or verdicts. The decidedly uneven treatment that public nuisance claims have received in the courts is yet another source of legal uncertainty and liability risk for developers whose models may cause widespread harm.

---

[162] Richard C. Ausness, *The Role of Litigation in the Fight Against Prescription Drug Abuse*, 116 W. Va. L. Rev. 1117, 1121 (2014).

[163] See Sharkey, *supra* note 58, for a detailed discussion of recovery for economic loss under public nuisance.

Chapter 7

The First Amendment and Section 230

So far, this report has focused on common-law tort doctrine rather than statutory or constitutional law. There are, however, certain constitutional provisions and statutory enactments that significantly influence the domain and operation of common-law tort liability. In this chapter, we briefly discuss two of them: the First Amendment to the U.S. Constitution, and Section 230 of the Communications Decency Act of 1996. First Amendment jurisprudence is an intricate and elaborate body of law, and its application to traditional software remains quite uncertain. Its application to novel and advanced AI systems is likely to exhibit even more uncertainty and complexity, and exactly how such considerations will play out in court cases is unclear. We do note, however, that common-law tort liability for AI model behavior that is not plausibly a form of "speech" (i.e., communicative or expressive in character) is less likely to implicate significant First Amendment concerns. Regarding Section 230, we conclude that while the application of the section to AI is as of yet unsettled, early indicators suggest that it will not prevent holding developers liable. However, both the First Amendment issues and the Section 230 issues discussed below warrant much deeper investigation than this report can provide.

First Amendment Considerations

In elaborating and refining common-law tort liability, the courts are often sensitive to First Amendment concerns regarding the effects of different possible liability rules on the production and limitation of speech.[164] Most famously, First Amendment concerns about unduly chilling speech led the Supreme Court to overhaul the common law of tort liability for defamation in *New York Times Co. v. Sullivan*,[165] and several cases that followed closely on its heels. In the name of the First Amendment, the Court remade defamation into a cause of action that can only be brought, in cases involving speech about public figures or matters of public concern, against *highly* culpable defendants.[166] The Court has similarly curtailed the invasion of privacy tort and the intentional

---

[164] For a helpful critical overview, see Kenneth S. Abraham & G. Edward White, *First Amendment Imperialism and the Constitutionalization of Tort Liability*, 98 Tex. L. Rev. 813 (2020).

[165] *New York Times Co. v. Sullivan*, 376 U.S. 254 (1964).

[166] *Restatement (Second) of Torts* § 580A (1977) ("One who publishes a false and defamatory communication concerning a public official or public figure in regard to his conduct, fitness or role in that capacity is subject to liability, if, but only if, he (a) knows that the statement is false and that it defames the other person, or (b) acts in reckless disregard of these matters.").

infliction of emotional distress tort on First Amendment grounds.[167] In line with the Supreme Court's solicitude for the First Amendment, lower courts have sometimes invoked free speech concerns to reason about the proper domain of other tort liability issues.[168]

Several of these decisions have potential implications for AI developer liability. In particular, courts are typically resistant to impose strict liability for the provision of ideas or information, even when it results in serious harm.[169] So, for example, the U.S. Court of Appeals for the Ninth Circuit barred plaintiffs who suffered severe food poisoning by relying on information in *The Encyclopedia of Mushrooms* from bringing strict products liability claims against its publishers.[170] The court maintained that publishers have no duty of care to investigate the veracity of the claims in the books they publish, and thus foreclosed the plaintiffs from recovering in negligence either. Similar judicial reasoning and instincts may preclude plaintiffs from recovering for injuries that derive from injuriously inaccurate information provided by advanced AI systems. Much may depend here on whether the developers of these systems are treated as "publishers" or another type of protected speaker.[171] If AI development is instead treated as an essentially nonexpressive activity—but rather an activity with certain informational by-products—common-law tort liability rules for injurious information provided by AI systems may instead be subject to less demanding forms of First Amendment scrutiny.[172]

Tort recovery will also probably be significantly easier to obtain when an AI system directly injures a plaintiff (e.g., by fraudulently deceiving her) or functions as a tool used by bad actors. So, for example, if a cyberterrorist directs a foundation model to construct and deploy a catastrophically harmful cyberweapon, the First Amendment will present less of a barrier to recovery than if the model had *instructed* the cyberterrorist on how to create such a weapon. The same will be true if a bioterrorist instructs an AI system to directly create a novel bioweapon (and subsequently deploys it). Put another way, tort recovery against the developers of AI models that directly act in the world to produce dangerous impacts may be much easier to obtain than tort recovery against the developers of machines that have injured plaintiffs purely through the provision of dangerous information.

A final source of legal uncertainty derives from the fact that, as a general matter, the First Amendment status of software code remains largely unclear. Lower courts have held that software code enjoys some degree of First Amendment protection, but the Supreme Court has never ruled directly on this question.[173] In addition, lower courts have not worked out *how much* First Amendment protection code enjoys, or whether it enjoys such protection even when it is serving an entirely

---

[167] *Restatement (Third) of Torts: Phys. & Emot. Harm* § 46 cmt. f (2012).

[168] *Id.* § 7 cmt. d ("Courts display a significant tendency to protect media defendants who publish material, including written publications and entertainment (music, video games, and movies), from liability for physical harm either through no- or limited-duty rulings based on First Amendment concerns or, more directly, by holding that the First Amendment provides a defense to such claims unless the communication rises to the level of incitement required by Brandenburg v. Ohio, 395 U.S. 444, 447 (1969).").

[169] *See generally* Marshall S. Shapo, *Shapo on the Law of Products Liability* (7th ed. 2017), 12–237.

[170] *Winter v. G.P. Putman's Sons*, 938 F.2d 1033, 1035 (9th Cir. 1991).

[171] *See, e.g.,* Eugene Volokh et al., *Freedom of Speech and AI Output*, 3 J. Free Speech L. 113 (2023).

[172] For an argument to this effect, see Peter Salib, *AI Outputs Are Not Protected Speech*, Wash. U. L. Rev. (forthcoming).

[173] *See* Xiangnong Wang, "De-Coding Free Speech: A First Amendment Theory for the Digital Age," Wis L. Rev. 169 1376 (2021) (citing Kyle Langvardt, *The Doctrinal Toll of Information as Speech*, 47 Loy U. Chi. L.J. 761, 775 [2016]).

functional rather than expressive purpose (e.g., when it is used to administer a server).[174] Even if traditional software code enjoys substantial First Amendment protection—because of its capacity to express or communicate the cognitive processes of software developers—critical components of an AI model may not be relevantly analogous. One of a model's key components, its weights, is derived through a trial-and-error process that is somewhat akin to evolutionary selection. Model weights are largely inscrutable to both their developers and everyone else.[175] For these reasons, it is plausible to maintain, model weights do not embody conscious design choices on the part of the model's developers and have little if any expressive or communicative import. There is a plausible (albeit contestable) argument, therefore, that model weights enjoy even less First Amendment protection than computer code, or even (perhaps) no First Amendment protection at all. Finally, it is worth noting that important components of the First Amendment analysis might rely on the purpose for which model developers make their code available or accessible to others.[176]

The Application of Section 230 to AI

The scope of AI developer liability may also be influenced by Section 230 of the Communications Decency Act of 1996, in which Congress mandated that "[n]o provider or user of an interactive computer service shall be treated as the publisher or speaker of any information provided by another information content provider."[177] Section 230 has been a major presence in cases against social media companies. Courts have relied on it to provide wide-ranging protection from liability to hosts of user-made content.[178]

Courts have not decided whether a firm that provides API access to an AI model that generates outputs resembling human-created content is covered by the Section 230 liability shield.[179] Some academic commentators (as well as Justice Gorsuch, in offhand comments during an oral argument) have answered largely in the negative.[180] Others answer in the positive or offer more complex and more uncertain analyses.[181] The answer may depend on whether such developers are "content creators" for the purposes of the statute, which would deprive them of its protection.

---

[174] *Id.* at 1387–88.

[175] See Michael Nielsen, *Neural Networks and Deep Learning* (2019), for an in-depth discussion of model training and the interoperability of the resulting weights.

[176] *See* Robert Post, *Encryption Source Code and the First Amendment*, 15 Berk. Tech. L.J. 713, 720 (2000) ("The author of encryption software who distributes encryption source code to consumers" to enable them to slip a disk into computers and thereby encrypt their messages is "not participating in public dialogue or debate" and, "[f]or this reason, regulation of encryption software in such contexts . . . appears, on its face, no different than the regulation of hardware in computers.").

[177] 47 U.S.C. § 230(c)(1).

[178] *See generally* Cong. Rsch. Serv., *Section 230: An Overview* (R46751, 2021).

[179] Section 230 is unlikely to apply to a developer that transfers an AI model to another party who then hosts it, as this would likely fail to qualify as providing an "interactive computer service" under the provision.

[180] *See, e.g.*, Matt Perault, *Section 230 Won't Protect ChatGPT*, 3 J. Free Speech L. 363 (2023); Transcript of Oral Argument, at 49, *Gonzalez v. Google*, 598 US__(2023).

[181] *See, e.g.*, Derek Bambauer & Mihai Surdeanu, *Authorbots*, 3 J. Free Speech L. 375 (2023); Jess Miers, *Yes, Section 230 Should Protect ChatGPT and Other Generative AI Tools*, Techdirt (Nov. 7, 2023).

However, this analysis of Section 230 as well as our analysis of the application of the First Amendment is preliminary, and both topics deserve a deeper investigation than can be provided here. An expansive application of either doctrine to AI could significantly limit the availability of tort claims for AI-caused damage. For this reason, policymakers, courts, and scholars will need to carefully consider the proper scope of these doctrines in this novel context.

Chapter 8

Conclusion

Highly capable AI systems are a growing presence in widely used consumer products, industrial and military enterprise, and critical societal infrastructure. Such systems may soon become a significant presence in tort cases as well—especially if their ability to engage in autonomous or semi-autonomous behavior, or their potential for harmful misuse, grows over the coming years.[182]

We have discussed several key points about AI developer liability that lawyers, judges, researchers, AI developers, policymakers, and others may wish to keep in mind:

- Tort law applies to AI developers, by default, since it applies by default to parties who engage in activities that pose risks of physical injury or property damage.
- AI developers whose models cause such injury or damage face significant liability exposure, under existing tort law, even if no legislation or regulation that specifically governs AI development is ever enacted. Developers may incur such liability under negligence doctrine as well as products liability and public nuisance doctrine.
- Tort law is an especially potent source of liability risk for developers that fail to avail themselves of industry-leading safety practices, for such developers are especially likely to be found negligent.
- In this way, and others, tort law provides AI developers with significant incentives to take care in developing and releasing advanced AI systems. By taking due care, developers can reduce the risk that their activities will cause harm to other people and reduce the risk that they will be held liable if their activities *do* cause such harm.

However, there remain significant interpretive uncertainties about the scope of developers' tort liability, particularly for harms committed by third parties using their models. It is also uncertain how important constitutional and statutory provisions, such as the First Amendment of the U.S. Constitution and Section 230 of the Communications Decency Act, may shape or limit developers' common-law tort liability. These areas of uncertainty are ripe for additional analysis and research to better inform policymakers about the intersection of tort law and AI.

Policymakers might choose to resolve some of these uncertainties by passing statutes that clarify or modify the common law of tort liability, as it applies to AI development. For example, policymakers might choose to alter or flesh out developers' duties of care, clarify the significance of industry best practices, modify the standards for proof of causation, or clarify or modify the conditions of developer liability for third-party modification or misuse of their models. Such interventions could help alleviate

---

[182] On the former, see Yonadav Shavit et al., *Practices for Governing Agentic AI Systems*, OpenAI (2023); and Alan Chan et al., *Harms from Increasingly Agentic Systems*, arXiv (2023).

the uncertainties faced by AI developers and the public and provide clarity on how tort law should treat large-scale AI harms.

However, legislators should be aware of the unique value that the common-law tort system embodies. The common law of torts imperfectly embeds a great deal of accumulated legal learning, and societal experience, regarding the governance of safety risks.[183] Moreover, partly because common-law tort standards skew toward generality rather than clear and detailed specificity, the common law of torts might prove to be more flexible and responsive to changing technological circumstances, and our rapidly evolving stock of knowledge about the nature and magnitude of AI safety risks, than more specific statutory requirements. Finally, with respect to some important issues in tort doctrine (such as the issue of negligence liability for third-party misuse), the common law's unsettled character may reflect the difficulty of formulating adequate general principles to handle the issue in question, requiring policymakers to carefully consider the evolving tort law doctrine in the courts. Whether and how it would be desirable to modify the common law of torts, as it applies to AI development, is a matter that warrants careful consideration as AI developers, researchers, policymakers, and the wider public discuss the future of AI governance.

---

[183] *See generally* Mariano-Florentino Cuellar, *A Common Law for the Age of Artificial Intelligence: Incremental Adjudication, Institutions, and Relational Non-Arbitrariness*, 119 Colum. L. Rev. 1773 (2019).

References

Abraham, Kenneth S., *Custom, Noncustomary Practice, and Negligence*, 109 Colum. L. Rev. 1784 (2009).

Abraham, Kenneth S., *Forms and Functions of Tort Law* (5th ed. 2017).

Abraham, Kenneth S., & Daniel Schwarcz, *Courting Disaster: The Underappreciated Risk of a Cyber-Insurance Catastrophe*, 27 Conn. Ins. L.J. 407 (2021).

Abraham, Kenneth S., & Catherine M. Sharkey, *The Glaring Gap in Tort Theory*, 133 Yale L.J. 2165 (2024).

Abraham, Kenneth S., & G. Edward White, *First Amendment Imperialism and the Constitutionalization of Tort Liability*, 98 Tex. L. Rev. 813 (2020).

AI Safety Inst., Advanced AI Evaluations at AISI: May Update (May 20, 2024), https://www.aisi.gov.uk/work/advanced-ai-evaluations-may-update.

American Law of Products Liability (Russell J. Davis et al., eds., 3d ed. 1987).

Anderson, Nate, Confirmed: US and Israel Created Stuxnet, Lost Control of It, Ars Technica blog (June 1, 2012, 6:00 AM), https://arstechnica.com/tech-policy/2012/06/confirmed-us-israel-created-stuxnet-lost-control-of-it/.

Anthropic, *The Claude 3 Model Family: Opus, Sonnet, Haiku* 3 (2024), https://www-cdn.anthropic.com/de8ba9b01c9ab7cbabf5c33b80b7bbc618857627/ Model_Card_Claude_3.pdf.

Anthropic, *Third-Party Testing as a Key Ingredient of AI Policy* (March 25, 2024), https://www.anthropic.com/news/third-party-testing.

Ausness, Richard C., *The Role of Litigation in the Fight Against Prescription Drug Abuse*, 116 W. Va. L. Rev. 1117 (2014).

Baker, Tom, *Liability Insurance as Tort Regulation: Six Ways That Liability Insurance Shapes Tort Law in Action*, 12 Conn. Ins. L.J. 1 (2005).

Bambauer, Derek, & Mihai Surdeanu, *Authorbots*, 3 J. Free Speech L. 375 (2023).

Bengio, Yoshua, et al., *Managing AI Risks in an Era of Rapid Progress*, 384 Science 842 (2024).

Bhatt, Manish, et al., *Purple Llama CyberSecEval: A Secure Coding Benchmark for Language Models*, arXiv 1 (2023), https://arxiv.org/pdf/2312.04724.pdf.

Black's Law Dictionary (11th ed. 2019).

Bloxham v. Glock Inc., 53 P.3d 196 (Ct. App. Ariz. 2002).

Bommasani, Rishi, et al., *On the Opportunities and Risks of Foundation Models*, arXiv (2022), https://arxiv.org/abs/2108.07258.

Bran, Andres M., et al., *ChemCrow: Augmenting Large-Language Models with Chemistry Tools*, arXiv (2024), https://arxiv.org/abs/2304.05376.

Branham v. Ford Motor Co., 701 S.E.2d 5 (S.C. 2010).

Bridges v. Parrish, 742 S.E.2d 794 (2013).

Britton v. Wooten, 817 S.W.2d 443 (Ky. 1991).

Bucknall, Benjamin S., & Robert F. Trager, *Structured Access for Third-Party Safety Research on Frontier AI Models Investigating Researchers' Model Access Requirements* (GovAI and Oxford Martin Sch. Working Paper, 2023).

Burkett v. Freedom Arms, Inc., 704 P.2d 118, 121 (Or. 1985).

CACI No. 1245. Affirmative Defense—Product Misuse or Modification.

Cardi, W. Jonathan, *Purging Foreseeability: The New Vision and Judicial Power in the Proposed Restatement (Third) of Torts*, 58 Vand. L. Rev. 739 (2005).

Carrington, Paul D., *The Consequences of Asbestos Litigation*, 26 Rev. Litig. 740 (2007).

Casey, Anthony J., & Joshua C. Macey, *In Defense of Chapter 11 for Mass Torts*, 90 U. Chi. L. Rev. 973 (2023).

Center for AI Safety, *Statement on AI Risk*, https://www.safe.ai/statement-on-ai-risk (last visited Nov. 7, 2023).

Chan, Alan, et al., *Harms from Increasingly Agentic Systems*, arXiv (2023), https://arxiv.org/abs/2302.10329.

City of Chicago v. Beretta U.S.A. Corp., 821 N.E.2d 1099 (Ill. 2004).

City of Cincinnati v. Beretta U.S.A. Corp., 768 N.E.2d 1136 (Ohio 2002).

City of Gary ex rel. King v. Smith & Wesson Corp., 801 N.E.2d 1222 (Ind. 2003).

Communications Decency Act, Pub. L. No. 104-104, Tit. V, 110 Stat. 133 (1996) (codified at 47 U.S.C. § 230(c)(1) (2012)).

Cong. Rsch. Serv., *Federal Admiralty and Maritime Jurisdiction Part 4: Torts and Maritime Contracts or Services* (LSB10827, 2022).

Cong. Rsch. Serv., *Introduction to Tort Law* (IF11291, 2023).

Cong. Rsch. Serv., *Section 230: An Overview* (R46751, 2021).

Craig v. Driscoll, 262 Conn. 312, 813 A.2d 1003 (2003).

Crootof, Rebecca, *The Internet of Torts: Expanding Civil Liability Standards to Address Corporate Remote Interference*, 69 Duke L.J. 583 (2019).

Cuellar, Mariano-Florentino, *A Common Law for the Age of Artificial Intelligence: Incremental Adjudication, Institutions, and Relational Non-Arbitrariness*, 119 Colum. L. Rev. 1773 (2019).

Deng, Jiangyi, et al., *SOPHON: None-Fine-Tunable Learning to Restrain Task Transferability for Pre-Trained Models*, arXiv (2024), https://arxiv.org/abs/2404.12699.

Devlin, Jacobin, et al., *BERT: Pre-Training of Deep Bidirectional Transformers for Language Understanding*, arXiv (2019),
https://arxiv.org/abs/1810.04805.

Dobbs, Dan B., et al., *The Law of Torts* (2d ed. 2011).

Erie Railroad Co. v. Tompkins, 304 U.S. 64 (1938).

Fang, Richard, et al., *LLM Agents Can Autonomously Exploit One-Day Vulnerabilities*, arXiv (2024),
https://arxiv.org/abs/2404.08144.

Gade, Pranav, et al., *BadLlama: Cheaply Removing Safety Fine-Tuning from Llama 2-Chat 13B*, arXiv (2023),
https://arxiv.org/abs/2311.00117.

Galanter, Matt, *The Vanishing Trial: An Examination of Trials and Related Matters in Federal and State Courts*, 1 J. of Empirical Legal Stud. 459 (2004).

Geistfeld, Mark, *Legal Ambiguity, Liability Insurance, and Tort Reform*, 60 DePaul L. Rev. 539 (2011).

Geistfeld, Mark, *Products Liability* (2d ed. 2021).

Geistfeld, Mark, A., *A Roadmap for Autonomous Vehicles: State Tort Liability, Automobile Insurance, and Federal Safety Regulation*, 105 Calif. L. Rev. 1611 (2017).

Geistfeld, Mark, *Strict Products Liability 2.0: The Triumph of Judicial Reasoning over Mainstream Tort Theory*, 14 J. Tort L. 403 (2021).

Geistfeld, Mark, *Tort Law in the Age of Statutes*, 99 Iowa L. Rev. 957 (2013).

Gemini Team, Google, *Gemini: A Family of Highly Capable Multimodal Models*, arXiv 29 (2023),
https://arxiv.org/abs/2312.11805.

Gergen, Mark P., *The Jury's Role in Deciding Normative Issues in the American Common Law*, 68 Fordham L. Rev. 407 (1999).

Gerstein, Daniel M., & Erin N. Leidy, *Emerging Technology and Risk Analysis: Artificial Intelligence and Critical Infrastructure*, Homeland Security Operational Analysis Center operated by RAND, RR-A2873-1, 2024. As of June 14, 2024:
https://www.rand.org/pubs/research_reports/RRA2873-1.html

Giffords Law Center, *Gun Industry Immunity*,
https://giffords.org/lawcenter/gun-laws/policy-areas/other-laws-policies/gun-industry-immunity/ (last visited Jan. 30, 2024).

Gilles, Stephen G., *The Invisible Hand Formula*, 80 Va. L. Rev. 1015 (1994).

Goodwin, Michael, *What Is an API?*, IBM,
https://www.ibm.com/topics/api (last visited Nov. 7, 2023).

Gross, Samuel R., & Kent D. Syverud, *Don't Try: Civil Jury Verdicts in a System Geared to Settlement*, 44 UCLA L. Rev. 1 (1996).

Hamilton v. Beretta U.S.A. Corp., 750 N.E.2d 1055, opinion after certified question answered, 264 F.3d 21 (2d Cir. 2001).

Henderson, Peter, et al., *Self-Destructing Models: Increasing the Costs of Harmful Dual Uses of Foundation Models*, arXiv (2022), https://arxiv.org/abs/2211.14946.

In re DePuy Orthopaedics, Inc., Pinnacle Hip Implant Prod. Liab. Litig., 888 F.3d 753 (5th Cir. 2018).

In re Sept. 11 Litig., 280 F. Supp. 2d 279 (S.D.N.Y. 2003).

Intellect Art Multimedia, Inc. v. Milewski, 899 N.Y.S.2d 60, 2009 WL 2915273 (Sup. Ct. 2009).

Kendrick, Leslie, *The Perils and Promise of Public Nuisance*, 132 Yale L.J. 702 (2023).

Kinniment, Megan, et al., *Evaluating Language-Model Agents on Realistic Autonomous Tasks*, arXiv (2023), https://arxiv.org/abs/2312.11671.

Koenig, Thomas, *The Shadow Effect of Punitive Damages on Settlements*, Wis. L. Rev. 169 (1998).

Legal Information Institute, *Restatement of the Law* (Aug. 2020), https://www.law.cornell.edu/wex/restatement_of_the_law.

Lerment, Simon, et al., *LoRA Fine-Tuning Efficiently Undoes Safety Training in Llama 2-Chat 70B*, arXiv (2023), https://arxiv.org/abs/2310.20624.

MacPherson v. Buick Motor Co., 217 N.Y. 382, 384, 111 N.E. 1050 (1916).

Maloy, Richard, *Forum Shopping? What's Wrong with That?*, 24 QLR 25 (2005).

Maynard v. Snapchat, Inc., 870 S.E.2d 739 (Ga. 2022).

Miers, Jess, *Yes, Section 230 Should Protect ChatGPT and Other Generative AI Tools*, Techdirt (Nov. 7, 2023), https://www.techdirt.com/2023/03/17/yes-section-230-should-protect-chatgpt-and-others-generative-ai-tools/.

Minhee, Christine, *States' Opioid Settlement Statuses*, Opioid Settlement Tracker, https://www.opioidsettlementtracker.com/globalsettlementtracker (last visited Jan. 30, 2024).

Morris, Clarence, *Custom and Negligence*, 42 Colum. L. Rev. 1147 (1942).

Mouton, Christopher A., Caleb Lucas, & Ella Guest, *The Operational Risks of AI in Large-Scale Biological Attacks: A Red-Team Approach*, RAND, RR-A2977-1, 2023. As of June 14, 2024: https://www.rand.org/pubs/research_reports/RRA2977-1.html

New York Times Co. v. Sullivan, 376 U.S. 254 (1964).

Nielsen, Michael, *Neural Networks and Deep Learning*, Determination Press, 2019.

OpenAI, *Disrupting Malicious Uses of AI by State-Affiliated Threat Actors* (Feb. 11, 2024), https://openai.com/index/disrupting-malicious-uses-of-ai-by-state-affiliated-threat-actors.

OpenAI, *GPT-4 System Card* 15 (2023), https://cdn.openai.com/papers/gpt-4-system-card.pdf.

Oversight of A.I.: Principles for Regulation Before the Subcomm. on Privacy, Tech. and the Law of H. Comm. On the Judiciary, 118th Cong. (2023) (Written Testimony of Dario Amodei, Ph.D., Co-Founder and CEO, Anthropic), https://www.judiciary.senate.gov/imo/media/doc/2023-07-26_-_testimony_-_amodei.pdf.

Owen, David G., *Design Defect Ghosts*, 74 Brook L. Rev. 927 (2009).

Owen, David G., & Mary J. Davis, *Owen & Davis on Products Liability* (4th ed. 2022).

Patwardhan, Tejal, et al., *Building an Early Warning System for LLM-Aided Biological Threat Creation* (2024), https://openai.com/index/building-an-early-warning-system-for-llm-aided-biological-threat-creation.

Perault, Matt, *Section 230 Won't Protect ChatGPT*, 3 J. Free Speech L. 363 (2023).

Perline, Kellin, et al., *Exploiting Novel GPT-4 APIs*, arXiv (2023), https://arxiv.org/abs/2312.14302.

Phipps v. General Motors Corp., 363 A.2d 955 (Md. 1976).

Phuong, Mary, et al., *Evaluating Frontier Models for Dangerous Capabilities*, arXiv (2024), https://arxiv.org/abs/2403.13793.

Pitts v. Genie Indus., Inc., 921 N.W.2d 597 (Neb. 2019).

Posner, Richard A., *A Theory of Negligence*, 1 J. Legal Stud. 29 (1972).

Post, Robert, *Encryption Source Code and the First Amendment*, 15 Berk. Tech. L.J. 713 (2000).

Press Release, U.K. Dept. of Sci., Innovation, and Tech, New Commitment to Deepen Work on Severe AI Risks Concludes AI Seoul Summit (May 22, 2024), https://www.gov.uk/government/news/new-commitmentto-deepen-work-on-severe-ai-risks-concludes-ai-seoul-summit.

Press Release, The White House, Biden-Harris Administration Secures Voluntary Commitments from Leading Artificial Intelligence Companies to Manage the Risks Posed by AI (July 21, 2023).

Press Release, The White House, President Biden Issues Executive Order on Safe, Secure, and Trustworthy Artificial Intelligence (Oct. 30, 2023).

Protection of Lawful Commerce in Arms Act, Pub. L. No. 109-92, 119 Stat. 2095 (2005) (codified at 15 U.S.C. §§ 7901-03 [2018]).

Pure Economic Loss in Europe (Mauro Bussani & Vernon Valentine Palmer, eds., 2003).

Qi, Xiangyu, et al., *Fine-Tuning Aligned Language Models Compromises Safety, Even When Users Do Not Intend To!*, arXiv (2023), https://arxiv.org/abs/2310.03693.

Restatement of Torts, 4 vols. (Am. L. Inst. 1934–39).

Restatement (Second) of Torts, 4 vols. (Am. L. Inst. 1965–79).

Restatement (Third) of Torts: Physical and Emotional Harm, 2 vols. (Am. L. Inst. 2010–12).

Restatement (Third) of Torts: Products Liability (Am. L. Inst. 1998).

Restatement (Third) of Torts: Remedies (Tentative Draft No. 2) (Am. L. Inst. 2023).

Robinson v. Reed-Prentice Div. of Package Mach. Co., 403 N.E.2d 440 (N.Y. 1980).

Rodgers v. Christie, 795 Fed. App'x 878 (3d Cir. Mar. 6, 2020).

Salib, Peter, *AI Outputs Are Not Protected Speech*, Wash. U. L. Rev. (forthcoming).

Sandbrink, Jonas B., *Artificial Intelligence and Biological Misuse: Differentiating Risks of Language Models and Biological Design Tools*, arXiv (2023), https://arxiv.org/abs/2306.13952.

Scheurer, Jeremy, et al., *Language Models Can Strategically Deceive Their Users When Put Under Pressure*, arXiv (2023), https://arxiv.org/abs/2311.07590.

Schwartz, Gary T., *The Myth of the Ford Pinto Case*, 43 Rutgers L. Rev. 1013 (1991).

Seger, Elizabeth, et al., *Open-Sourcing Highly Capable Foundation Models: An Evaluation of Risks, Benefits, and Alternative Methods for Pursuing Open-Source Objectives*, arXiv 6 (2023), https://arxiv.org/abs/2311.09227.

Shapo, Marshall S., *Shapo on the Law of Products Liability* (7th ed. 2017).

Sharkey, Catherine M., *Public Nuisance as Modern Business Tort: A New Unified Framework for Liability for Economic Harms*, 70 DePaul L. Rev. 431 (2020).

Shavit, Yonadav, et al., *Practices for Governing Agentic AI Systems*, OpenAI (2023), https://cdn.openai.com/papers/practices-for-governing-agentic-ai-systems.pdf.

Shevlane, Toby, *Structured Access: An Emerging Paradigm for Safe AI Deployment*, arXiv 1 (2022), https://arxiv.org/abs/2201.05159. .

Shevlane, Toby, et al., *Model Evaluation for Extreme Risks*, arXiv (2023), https://arxiv.org/abs/2305.15324.

Solaiman, Irene, *The Gradient of Generative AI Release: Methods and Considerations*, arXiv (2023), https://arxiv.org/abs/2302.04844.

Steiner, Eva, *French Law: A Comparative Approach* (2d ed. 2018).

Strauss v. Belle Realty Co., 482 N.E.2d 34, 36 (N.Y. 1985).

Symeonides, Symeon C., *Choice of Law* (2016).

The T.J. Hooper v. Northern Barge Corp., 60 F.2d 737 (2d Circ. 1932).

Transcript of Oral Argument, *Gonzalez v. Google LLC* 598 US (2023).

Twerski, Aaron, & J.A. Henderson, *Achieving Consensus on Defective Product Design*, 83 Cornell L. Rev. 867 (1998).

U.K. Dept. of Sci., Innovation & Tech., *Emerging Processes for Frontier AI Safety* (Policy Paper, Oct. 27, 2023). https://assets.publishing.service.gov.uk/media/653aabbd80884d000df71bdc/emerging-processes -frontier-ai-safety.pdf.

U.K. Dept. of Sci., Innovation & Tech., *Introducing the AI Safety Institute* (Policy Paper, Nov. 2, 2023), https://www.gov.uk/government/publications/ai-safety-institute-overview/introducing-the-ai-safety -institute#definitions.

U.S. Dept. of Comm., U.S. Secretary of Commerce Gina Raimondo Releases Strategic Vision on AI Safety, Announces Plan for Global Cooperation Among AI Safety Institutes (May 21, 2024), https://www.commerce.gov/news/press-releases/2024/05/us-secretary-commerce-gina-raimondo -releases-strategic-vision-ai-safety.

U.S. Dept. of Justice, *Punitive Damage Awards in State Courts, 2005* (2011).

U.S. v. Carroll Towing, 159 F.2d 169 (2d Cir. 1947).

Volokh, Eugene, et al., *Freedom of Speech and AI Output*, 3 J. Free Speech L. 113 (2023).

Wang, Xiangnong, *De-Coding Free Speech: A First Amendment Theory for the Digital Age*, Wis. L. Rev. 1373 (2021).

Watkins v. Ford Motor Co., 190 F.3d 1213 (11th Cir. 1999).

Watson v. Kentucky & Indiana Bridge & R. Co., 137 Ky. 619, *modified sub nom.*

Watson v. Kentucky & I. Bridge & R. Co., 137 Ky. 619 (1910), and abrogated by *Britton v. Wooten, 817 S.W.2d 443* (Ky. 1991).

Wei, Alexander, et al., *Jailbroken: How Does LLM Safety Training Fail?*, arXiv 9 (2023), https://arxiv.org/abs/2307.02483.

Winter v. G.P. Putman's Sons, 938 F.2d 1033 (9th Cir. 1991).

Young v. Bryco Arms, 821 N.E.2d 1078 (Ill. 2004).

Zaza v. Marquess & Nell, Inc., 675 A.2d 620 (N.J. 1996).

Zhan, Qiusi, et al., *Removing RLHF Protections in GPT-4 via Fine-Tuning*, arXiv (2024), https://arxiv.org/abs/2311.05553.